THE ORAL LAW DEBUNKED

~ Debunking the myth of Rabbinic Oral Law ~

Dedicated to all other Jewish believers in Yeshua

ISBN: 9781793227560

Published by: ONE FOR ISRAEL Ministry
(www.oneforisrael.org)

ONE FOR ISRAEL

CONTENTS

Introduction

The intention of the authors of this short book is to present a vigorous critique of traditional-rabbinic Judaism. It should be clearly stated at the outset, however, that this critique is offered in the context of an intramural discussion between Jews who believe in Yeshua (Jesus) and those who do not yet follow Him. It should not be understood as an attack on the Jewish people, but rather as a dispute between different sects within Judaism, over the true interpretation of the Tanakh and the authority thereof.

This paper's main objective will be to examine the validity of the following premise: for two millennia Judaism has been held hostage under the government and philosophy of one distinct sect, namely the Pharisees and their heirs—the rabbis. Since the destruction of the Second Temple, biblical Judaism had ceased to exist and the rabbinic traditions took over, with a completely reformed version of Judaism which centered on three main pillars: the rabbis themselves, the yeshiva (ישיבה) and the Halacha (הלכה). This work will also try to examine how this sect managed to enforce its traditions upon Israel and at what cost.

In order to establish their authority over the Jewish people, the rabbis came up with the revolutionary idea according to which their philosophy, traditions and teachings (i.e., the Oral Law) were passed on through the generations, beginning with Moses and ultimately with God Himself.[1] Henceforth, the focus of the rabbinic religion has been to study and meditate on the Oral Law (Oral Law). In fact, the Oral Law serves as the foundation upon which all the traditions of rabbinic Judaism stand. Without the rabbis' traditions, rabbinic Judaism losses all its validity and existence.[2] In other words, *if the divine origin of the Oral Law is nothing but a myth, then rabbinic Judaism has no leg to stand on.*[3]

Other main objectives of this paper would be to historically examine how the sect of the Pharisees was able to attain such a stronghold over Judaism, to investigate whether the Oral Law's traditions are in fact rooted in the Bible and genuinely reflect God's will for men, and to examine the implications of the Oral Law on Judaism today, especially in regard to Israel's relationship to the New Testament and Yeshua. The first chapter of this paper will deal with the advent of the Pharisees and the circumstances which brought them into the position of authority.

---

[1]Mishna, T. Avot 1:1. See further discussion at: Albeck, Shalom (in Hebrew):
שלום אלבק, מבוא למשפט העברי בימי התלמוד, הוצאת אוניברסיטת בר אילן, 1999, עמ' 17

[2]See: Zvi Kortzville, in: Yosef Ofer (ed.), "The method of examinations of Rabbi Breuer" (In Hebrew):
צבי קורצווייל, בתוך: יוסף עופר (עורך), 'שיטת הבחינות' של הרב מרדכי ברויאר, בהוצאת: תבונות, 2005, עמ' 267

[3]Michael Brown, in: Sid Roth, ed., *They Thought for Themselves*, 1996. Hebrew version: (Tel-Aviv: Maoz, 2001), 31.

Chapter 1

THE ANCESTORS OF THE RABBIS

For over a millennium, “Judaism” has been identified with the rabbinic traditions and vice versa.[4] Who were the rabbis; where did they originate; what did they believe; and what was their agenda? The rabbis were leaders of a sect that succeeded the Pharisees.[5] The Pharisees were one of three major sects (or groups) which were founded and operated during the period of the Second Temple, along with the Sadducees and the Essenes.[6]

The Pharisees did not become a distinct group earlier than the year 150 BC, because their name (פרושים, in Hebrew) does not appear anywhere earlier; and moreover, other sources,

---

[4]David Flusser, *The Dead Sea Scrolls and the Essenes* (In Hebrew):
דוד פלוסר, מגילות מדבר יהודה והאיסיים, בהוצאת: משרד הביטחון, רעננה, 1985, עמ' 14

[5]Elisha Qimron, The Dead Sea Scrolls – The Hebrew Writings, Oral Law. 1 (In Hebrew):
אלישע קימרון, מגילות מדבר יהודה: החיבורים העבריים - כרך ראשון, בהוצאת: יד יצחק בן-צבי, ירושלים, 2010, עמ' 243

[6]Flusser, *The Religion of Israel in the Second Temple Period* (in Hebrew):
פלוסר, ד., דת ישראל בתקופת בית שני, בתוך: אבי-יונה, מ. וברס, צ. (עורכים), ההיסטוריה של עם ישראל - חברה ודת בימי בית שני, ירושלים, הוצאה לאור עם עובד, 1983

later than 150 BC, give the impression that the Pharisees, the Sadducees and the Essenes came to be at about this time and not earlier.[7] In fact, the Second Temple Period was the bed-rock upon which the Jewish theology, as we know it today, grew up and developed.[8]

Rabbinic literature documents four categorical obligations which a member of the Pharisees had to commit himself to keep:[9]

> שלא ליתן תרומות ומעשרות לעם הארץ; ושלא יעשה טהרות אצל עם הארץ; ושיהא אוכל חולין בטהרה; המקבל עליו להיות נאמן.[10]

Meaning: "Not to give donations and tithes to the people of the land;[11] and that he should not practice purity [laws] with the people of the land; and that he should eat the cholin in purity;[12] [and he should also] take upon himself to be loyal." This sect, which was formed during the Hasmonean period, has defined its members with the title "Chachamim" (חכמים, in Hebrew; which literally means "wise men"), and was

---

[7]Yigal I. Levin, "Political struggles between the Pharisees and the Sadducees", in Daniel R. Schwartz, (ed.), *Studies in Jewish History of the Second Temple Period* (in Hebrew):
לוין, י. ל., בתוך: דניאל שוורץ (עורך), מחקרים בתולדות ישראל בתקופת הבית השני, בהוצאת מרכז זלמן שזר לחקר תולדות העם היהודי, ירושלים, 1996, עמ' 290

[8]Flusser, *Judaism of Second Temple Period*, (in Hebrew):
דוד פלוסר, יהדות בית שני, חכמיה וספרותה, הוצאת מאגנס, ירושלים, 2002, עמ' 12

[9]Flusser, *The Religion of Israel in the Second Temple Period* (in Hebrew):
דוד פלוסר, מגילות מדבר יהודה והאיסיים, בהוצאת: משרד הביטחון, רעננה, 1985, עמ' 17

[10]Tosefta, Damai 2:2–3. Unless mentioned otherwise, all Hebrew quotes of rabbinic literature are taken from Mechon-Mamre's website, at: http://www.mechon-mamre.org/b/b0.htm

[11]The rabbinic term, "people of the land" (עם הארץ, in Hebrew), carries a rather negative meaning and refers to someone in Israel "who has sons, but does not raise them up to learn the [Oral] Torah" (b. Talmud, Sota 22a; Brachot 47b).

[12]The rabbinic term "eat the cholin in purity," means to purify any kind of food or dishes before eating, including the washing of the hands etc. see Safrai, S. (1983: 130-131), in Hebrew:
שמואל ספראי, בשלהי הבית השני ובתקופת המשנה: פרקים בתולדות החברה והתרבות, בהוצאת: מרכז זלמן שזר לחקר תולדות העם היהודי ישראל, ירושלים, 1983, עמ' 130–131

known for passing its wisdom orally.[13] According to the Oral Law, they continue a tradition that was given to Moses on Mount Sinai,[14] and in fact, is even traced back to Adam.[15]

In the time of Herod the Great,[16] the sect of the Pharisees had consisted of 6,000 men.[17] Despite its small size, by 70 AD this sect managed to gain political, legal and religious control over the entire nation by ruling the Sanhedrin.[18]

---

[13]Rachel Elior, *Memory and Oblivion: The Secret of the Dead Sea Scrolls* (In Hebrew):
אליאור, ר., זיכרון ונשייה: סודן של מגילות מדבר יהודה, בהוצאת: מכון ון ליר בירושלים, הקיבוץ המאוחד, 2009, עמ' 148

[14]Mishna, T. Avot 1:1.

[15]ספר "עבודת הקודש" לרבי מאיר בן גבאי, חלק ג' פרק כ"א

[16]Herod was born around the year 73 BC and ruled Judea between the years 37 to 4 BC. See in Menachem Stern, *The Kingdom of Herod* (in Hebrew):
מנחם שטרן, מלכותו של הורדוס, בהוצאת: משרד הביטחון, רעננה, 1992, עמ' 113–114

[17]Flusser, *The Dead Sea Scrolls and the Essenes*, 18.

[18]Levin, I. L., in: Barkai, G. & Shiller, E. (eds.), Jerusalem in 2nd Temple period (in Hebrew):
לוין, י. ל., בתוך: גבריאל ברקאי ואלי שילר (עורכים), "אריאל: כתב עת לידיעת ארץ ישראל" - ירושלים בתפארתה: תולדות ירושלים בימי בית שני", 1996: 136–138

Chapter 2

GAME OF THRONES

Ultimately, it was a question of authority over the people Israel.[19] But how did the Pharisees manage to take the mandate, which was initially given by the Torah to the priests,[20] and claim it as their own? How did they become the absolute authority over Judaism? With the inevitable destruction of the Second Temple in 70 AD, the priests found themselves standing on unfamiliar ground concerning their authority and their daily livelihood; soon after, they had lost their leadership and prestige to the rabbis.[21] But the power struggles between the two sects started earlier.

A testimony to the fierce dispute between the leading sects of the Second Temple Period, is found in the Dead Sea Scrolls, where it is said about the Pharisees:

---

[19]Daniel Gruber, *Rabbi Akiba's Messiah: The Origins of Rabbinic Authority* (Tel Aviv: Maoz Israel, 2004), 324 (In the Hebrew version).

[20]See Elior, Memory and Oblivion – The Mystery of The Dead Sea Scrolls, (in Hebrew):
רחל אליאור, זיכרון ונשייה: סודן של מגילות מדבר יהודה, בהוצאת: מכון ון ליר בירושלים, הקיבוץ המאוחד, 2009: עמ' 150–153

[21]Gruber, *Rabbi Akiba's Messiah*, 213.

מתעי אפרים אשר בתלמוד שקרם ולשון כזביהם ושפת מרמה יתעו רבים.[22]

Meaning: “deceivers of Ephraim, which by their lies of teaching, tongue of falsehood and language of fraud will mislead many.” The leader of the Pharisees is described by the Dead Sea Scrolls as “the preacher of deception” (מטיף הכזב) and “the man of mockery” (איש הלצון) and he is accused of misleading many with his deceitful teachings,[23] and even of detesting the written Torah (מאס את התורה).[24]

The ancient historian Yosef ben-Matityahu (Josephus Flavius) reinforced this when he wrote that the Pharisees commanded Israel with traditional laws which were never a part of the written Torah, or written Law and therefore, were rejected by the Sadducees, who argued in favour of sticking to the text alone. In response, adds Josephus, fierce arguments and disputes broke out between the two sects.[25]

Josephus, along with several rabbinic writings, document the political rivalry between the King Alexander Yanai[26] and the Pharisees, which led to the crucifixion of eight hundred Pharisees.[27] That happened supposedly after the Pharisees invited the Slovakian King (המלך הסלוקי), to come and conquer Jerusalem from the hands of King Alexander

---

[22]Nitzan, B., in: Kister, M., (ed.), Qumran scrolls – Introduction and research (in Hebrew):
ניצן, ב., בתוך: מנחם קיסטר (עורך), מגילות קומראן מבואות ומחקרים - כרך ראשון, הוצאת: יד יצחק בן-צבי, ירושלים, 2009, עמ' 178

[23]Ibid., 192–194.

[24]Ibid., 178.

[25]Elior, 152–153.

[26]He ruled between the years 103–76 BC and supported the Sadducees, at the expense of the Pharisees. See Eyal Regev, *The Sadducees and their Halakha* (in Hebrew):
איל רגב, הצדוקים והלכתם: על דת וחברה בימי בית שני, בהוצאת: יד יצחק בן-צבי, ירושלים, 2005, עמ' 262–261

[27]Ibid., 262.

Yanai.[28] In fact, The Pharisees exploited the intensification of the inheritance struggles between the successors of Alexandra and Yanai; they deliberately invite the Romans in, to conquer Israel; and by doing so, to dismantle and eliminate the rule of the Hasmoneans, thus paving the way for the rabbinic leadership to take over.[29]

It was Queen Shlom-Tzion (known also as "Alexandra")[30] who was fond of the Pharisees and enabled them to expand their influence among the people of Israel.[31] During Alexandra's days, the Pharisees started spreading their teachings and imposing it even on those who opposed them. In fact, the establishment of the "Zugot" ([32]זוגות), was meant to establish the rule of Torah in Israel, not merely in a political form, but also in ways which mandate everyday conduct.[33]

At that point, the rivalry between the Pharisees and the Sadducees had been revealed in all its severity. Josephus wrote that Queen Alexandra gave the Pharisees full authority over the people and renewed all their traditional rulings (which had been abolished earlier by Hyrcanus, her father-in-

---

[28]Levin, I. L., in: Schwartz, D. R. (ed.), 295.

[29]Elam, Y., What Happened Here (in Hebrew):
יגאל עילם, מה התרחש כאן, בהוצאת: עם עובד, רעננה, 2012, עמ' 57–58

[30]Wife of King Alexander Yanai and the heir to the throne after his death. See Rapaport, U., in: Schwartz, D. R. (ed.), 283.

[31]Nitzan, B., in: Kister, M., (ed.), 179.

[32]"Zugot," literally means "pairs" and refers to the two sages which governed the Sanhedrin and presumably received the Oral Law from Moses. See: Maimonides, Introduction to Mishne Torah 4–22; and also: Werman, C. & Shemesh, A., Revealing the Hidden: Exegesis and Halakha in the Qumran Scrolls (in Hebrew):
ורמן, כ. ושמש, א., לגלות נסתרות: פרשנות והלכה במגילות קומראן, בהוצאת: מוסד ביאליק, ירושלים, 2011, עמ' 83–94

[33]Averbach, Moshe. Jewish Education During the Mishna and the Talmud (in Hebrew) :
משה אברבך, החינוך היהודי בתקופת המשנה והתלמוד, הוצאת ראובן מס בע"מ, ירושלים, 2008, עמ' 19

law).[34] Alexandra handed the priesthood over to Hyrcanus the II and the legal system over to the Pharisees.[35] This was an extremely important turning point for the Jewish world; the beginning of an era in which every new religious development in Judaism would carry a legal dimension.[36]

The Pharisees were the biggest opponents of the Sadducees' priesthood. In one instance they deliberately defiled a certain priest so he could no longer bring sacrifices; in another instance they ordered the stoning of a priest who dared to go against their teachings; one priest is even recorded saying that even though they, the Sadducees, had responsibility over the Temple, they still feared the Pharisees. Indeed, the Pharisees rejected and dismissed many of the procedures under which the Sadducees operated and enforced new traditions, to which the priests would have to be subject.[37]

After the Second Temple was destroyed, the Pharisees at last had the opportunity to implement their religious revolution, to create a national body which did not need a specific physical location to stand on[38]—a body which would be governed by their teachings and which could exist universally.[39]

In sharp contrast to the priests, the Pharisees denied both the dynastic system upon which the Sadducees inherited their

---

[34]Levin, I. L., in: Schwartz, D. R. (ed.), 291.

[35]Rapaport, U., in: Schwartz, D. R. (ed.), 283.
[36]Gruber, 435.

[37]Ibid., 206. See examples for Halachic disagreements between the Pharisees and the Sadducees in the Mishna, Yadaim 4:6–7.

[38]Schwartz, D. R., 414–15.

[39]Asher Zvi Hirsch Ginsberg (known by the pen name "Ahad Ha'am"), in Hebrew:
אחד העם, "בשר ורוח", בתוך: על פרשת דרכים, כרך ב', חלק שלישי, ברלין, 1921, עמ' 222-232

authority and their source of authority for divine knowledge. They rejected the exclusivity of the Sadducees as priests who served in the Temple. The rabbis also declared that prophecy had ceased to exist and the writings made by the priests were therefore null and void.[40] After the destruction of the Temple, they claimed authority to determine the schedule of feasts—an authority that had belonged to the priests until then.[41]

With the advent of the Oral Law, which was based on human reasoning, the Pharisees managed to push aside many of the values that had been reflected in the old priestly order. The rabbinic tradition was exempt from any sacred boundaries and thus had no preconditions; by using principles such as "laws of Moses from Sinai" (הלכה למשה בסיני) or "after many, turn" (אחרי רבים להטות), the Sages (חז"ל)[42] established a new model of judicial decision making, which was in complete contrast to the Written Law and stood in clear opposition to the priestly method.[43]

The rabbis finalized their religious domination by imposing severe censorship over the Bible through an interpretation by methods which would suit their agenda and further establish their authority. By the end of the first century AD, their victory over prophecy and priesthood was accomplished, and there was no turning back for nearly two millennia.[44]

---

[40]In fact, the rabbis turned the writings of the Sadducees and the Hasmoneans (חשמונאים) into the apocryphal books and forbade Israel to read them (Elior, 66, 71).

[41]Elior, 66, 132–33.

[42]The Sages (or חז"ל, in Hebrew), literally means: "our wise rabbis, blessed be their memory."

[43]Elior, 136–50.

[44]Averbach, 300.

It seems as if the destruction of the Second Temple gave the Pharisees exactly the opportunity they had hoped for. "Take Jerusalem, but give me Yavne and its scholars,"[45] begged Rabbi Yochanan Ben-Zakkai from Vespasian, and by doing so he determined the fate of the biblical Judaism, which had been, up to that point, based on the Temple and the priests.[46]

The Temple, it seems, was sacrificed upon the altar of tradition![47] Hence, Rabbi Akiba's support of Bar-Kokhba was a calculated step toward the goal of establishing the rabbis' revolution. The implications of the revolt in 135 AD finally eliminated the aspirations to any form of Judaism other than rabbinic.[48] The sages' religion flourished when the Jewish people were exiled—not in spite of the exile, but because of it. The rabbis could not have implemented their tradition, except through an uncompromising separation from the physical and earthly state of government, ruled by priests and kings.[49]

From here on, Judaism was total dependent upon the rabbis and their Oral Law; the Pharisees reformation was completed. Judaism was in their hands.[50]

---

[45]My paraphrase of the passage from b. Talmud, Gittin 56b (in Hebrew):
תן לי יבנה וחכמיה וגו'

[46]Shapira, Amnon, Jewish Religious Anarchism (in Hebrew):
אמנון שפירא, אנרכיזם יהודי דתי, הוצאת אוניברסיטת אריאל בשומרון, 2015, עמ' 197

[47]See discussion in: Beitner, A., Yavneh Stories – Visiting the Sick and Consoling Mourners (in Hebrew):
עזריה בייטנר, סיפורי יבנה: ביקור חולים וניחום אבלים, הוצאת אוניברסיטת בר אילן, 2011, עמ' 11–12

[48]See: Gruber, 435–36.

[49]Elam, 57.

[50]Beitner, 11.

Chapter 3

THE ADVENT OF THE ORAL LAW

The myth of an Oral Law having divine authority was not made unintentionally. On the contrary, it was a direct method by which the rabbis could keep themselves as the ultimate source of knowledge and thus create total dependency on their teachings alone.[51] Of course, the Oral Law was also the main tool by which the Pharisees could push the priests (and especially the Sadducees) from power.[52]

In a paradoxical way, the Oral Law refers to all the writings made by the Sages, both Halacha (rabbinic law) and Agada (rabbinic legends and Midrash). In fact, the paradox is even greater, because there is probably no other religious sect in the world which has such a vast "Oral Law" literature as the rabbinic tradition. According to the Sages, the Oral Law was not created in the Second Temple Period, but was only developed and established by the rabbis following that period;[53] they claimed it was given by Moses together with

[51]Schiffman, L. H., From Text to Tradition: A History of Second Temple and Rabbinic Judaism, Ktav Pub Inc, 1st edition, 1991, 15.

[52]Elior, 153–54.

[53]Flusser, 1983.

the Written Law.[54] The term Oral Law includes the Mishna, Tosefta, Talmud, Halacha, Verdicts (פוסקים), Agada, Midrash, Books of Ethics (ספרי מוסר),[55] and even what a contemporary wise student (תלמיד חכם) of yeshiva will say to his rabbi![56] In fact, the Sages took it one step further, and argued:

אפילו מה שתלמיד שואל לרב, אמר הקב"ה למשה אותה שעה.[57]

Meaning: Even today, whatever a disciple would ask his rabbi, God has already given the answer to Moses, at Mount Sinai. Thus, the Oral Law takes on a much broader meaning than just the Mishna and the Talmud; it is an organic judicial system of laws, which keeps expanding with new relevant rulings that fit the ever-changing circumstances.[58]

The first appearances of the term "Oral Law" takes place in the Babylonian Talmud, where it is explicitly mentioned in three different tractates. This is rather surprising for a text that one would expect to promote the novel idea of the Oral Law.[59] As mentioned, the most ancient written rabbinic documents are dated no earlier than the second and third century AD, and some say even towards the end of the first

---

[54]According to b. Talmud, Brachot 5a. See discussion in: Rosenberg, Shalom (in Hebrew): שלום רוזנברג, לא בשמים היא: תורה שבעל פה - מסורת וחידוש, בהוצאת: תבונות, 1997, עמ' 9–14

[55]See: Orbach, E. E. (in Hebrew):
א. א. אורבך, חז"ל – פרקי אמונות ודעות, בהוצאת י"ל מאגנס, 1976, עמ' 1
And also: Kitzur Shulchan Aruch (in Hebrew):
שלמה גאנצפריד, קיצור שולחן ערוך, הוצאת ספרים שי למורא, ירושלים, 2009, סימן כ"ז, ג', עמ' 104

[56]According to j. Talmud, Pea 13a; and Midrash V'Ikra Raba 22:1; See in: Mack, H., The Ancient Commentary On the Bible (in Hebrew): חננאל מאק, הפרשנות הקדומה למקרא, בהוצאת: משרד הביטחון, רעננה, 1993, עמ' 93–94

[57]Midrash Shmot Raba 47:1; see in: Rosenberg, 10.

[58]Roth, M., Orthodox Judaism – The Human Dimension (in Hebrew):
מאיר רוט, אורתודוקסיה הומאנית, בהוצאת: הקיבוץ המאוחד, רעננה, 2013, עמ' 165–173

[59]Gruber, 133–39. See also Werman, C. & Shemesh, A., 83–86.

millennium.[60] In other words, there is no written source, earlier than the second century AD which explicitly links the Pharisaic laws to the giving of the Torah (מתן תורה) at Mount Sinai.[61]

Nevertheless, in complete disregard of this fact—or perhaps precisely in light of it—the rabbis argued that Moses was not the only one who knew the Oral Law; according to their literature, all the great figures of the Bible used to study and meditate on it. Accordingly, Adam and Eve learned the Oral Law; Abraham, Isaac and Jacob studied in a yeshiva; and so also did Joshua, King David, and others.[62]

The value of studying the Oral Law is so great that according to the Talmud, even God Himself spends the first three hours of each day studying the Oral Law in heaven.[63] Therefore, the rabbis promised that God sits and learns with every wise disciple who studies the Oral Law.[64] In fact, the Talmud[65] records a dispute between God and the heavenly yeshiva of the righteous rabbis' souls (מתיבתא דרקיעא), over a certain skin lesion; God argued that the lesion was pure, but the rabbis disagreed. In order to resolve the dispute, Rav Bar-Nachmani was invited to heaven and declared in favour of God.[66]

---

[60]Elior, 153.

[61]Werman, C. & Shemesh, A., 87.

[62]This appears throughout the rabbinic literature (in Hebrew):
במדרש "תנא דבי אליהו" פרק ו', עמ' ס"ה; מדרש ויקרא רבא, פרשה ב'; בראשית רבה, פרשת תולדות י'; תלמוד ירושלמי, ספר "עבודת הקודש" לרבי מאיר בן גבאי, חלק ג, ;עירובין לב, ב, פרק ה, הלכה א; בבלי, מגילה ג' ע"א; בבלי, מועד קטן ט"ז ב' פרק כ"א

[63]b. Talmud, Avodah Zarah 3b.

[64]j. Talmud, Taanit 21a.

[65]b. Talmud, Babah Metzia 86a

As emphasized, the rabbinic religion was based totally on the Oral tradition.[67] Therefore, the Sages did all that was within their power to elevate its status among Israel and to persuade the people that there was absolutely nothing more important than to study the Oral Law (תלמוד תורה כנגד כולם) day and night, for as long as they lived.[68] Hence, rabbinic literature is full of praise for the importance and the virtues of the Oral Law, so much so that the actual act of learning it has become a value in and of itself.[69]

The rabbis argued that studying the Oral Law was greater than rebuilding the Temple, more significant than honouring ones parents and even greater than saving lives.[70] The rabbis' idea of Judaism was all about education,[71] so learning the Oral Law became nothing short of a holy and divine task.[72] Thus, studying the Oral Law became both the purpose for living[73] and a responsibility which would last throughout life.[74] Concerning the age in which one should start studying rabbinic teachings, the norm was to begin when the child had reached five years,[75] although some rabbis went so far as to

---

[66]Nevertheless, when Maimonides attended this dispute, he argued in favour of the rabbis and against God. See in: Navon, C., Teiku (in Hebrew):
חיים נבון, תיקו – 101 ויכוחים גדולים של היהדות, בהוצאת: ידיעות אחרונות וספרי חמד, 2014, עמ' 43–44

[67]See in: Brown, M. L., 6.

[68]See Wiesel, E., The Talmudic Soul (in Hebrew):
אלי ויזל, הנשמה התלמודית, בהוצאת: משכל (ידיעות ספרים), 2014, עמ' 372

[69]Mack, H., 92–93.

[70]b. Talmud, Megila 16b.

[71]Stern, E. (in Hebrew):
אליעזר שטרן, אישים וכיוונים, בהוצאת: אוניברסיטת בר-אילן, רמת גן, 1987, עמ' 15

[72]Saks, J., Educating Toward Meaningful Jewish Prayer, Edited by Yoel Finkelman, Atid, 2001.

[73]Midrash Avot D'Rabbi Natan 14:2.

[74]Sheranski, B. (in Hebrew):
שרנסקי, ב., החינוך החרדי בימינו – מורשת סיני בדורנו, בהוצאת משרד החינוך, התרבות והספורט, ירושלים, 1999

argue that teaching the Oral Law should start from birth and even when the baby is still in his mother womb.[76] This was done due to the belief that what is being taught in an early stage would remain in the mind forever.[77]

As mentioned, there is no rabbinic Judaism without the Oral Law, and there could not be an Oral Law without the rabbis to teach it. Therefore, when the Sages elevated the status of the Oral Law, they also elevated their own. They have sanctified themselves by turning their names into lucky charms, which one could say in times of trouble.[78] The rabbis demanded the honour of kings[79] and of God Himself.[80] They did not stop there, but taught that their sayings are more serious than the words of the prophets[81] and that a rabbi is better than a prophet.[82] Therefore they threatened that anyone who dared to disobey their rulings would be executed in this world and suffer in the world to come.[83]

Accordingly, those who did not send their sons to yeshiva and

---

[75]Mishna, Avot 5.

[76]Kanerfogel, E. (in Hebrew):
קנרפוגל, א., החינוך והחברה היהודית באירופה הצפונית בימי הביניים, הוצאת הקיבוץ המאוחד, תל-אביב, 2003.

[77]See b. Takmud shabat 21b (the rabbis used the term "גירסא דינוקא"). Actually, the j. Talmud records Rabbi Joshua's mother taking him in his crib to the yeshiva when he was still a baby, just so he could hear others studying the Oral-Law (tractate Yebemoth 8b).

[78]E.g., b. Talmud, Avodah Zarah 18a.

[79]Tur-Sinai, N. H. (in Hebrew):
נ.ה. טור-סיני, הלשון והספר: בעיות יסוד במדע הלשון ובמקורותיה הספרותיים - כרך הספר, בהוצאת: מוסד ביאליק, ירושלים, 1959, עמ' 391
In fact, the rabbis considered themselves kings in practice and demanded to be treated accordingly. See: Steinsaltz, Adin (in Hebrew):
עדין שטיינזלץ, מדריך לתלמוד, בהוצאת כתר, ירושלים, 2002, עמ' 24

[80]b. Talmud, Psachim 22b and 108a.

[81]j. Talmud, Brachot 8b.

[82]b.Talmud, Baba Batra 12a.

[83]b. Talmud Eruvin 21b.

refused to submit to the rabbis' authority, were designated with the offensive term: "am-ha'aretz" (עם-הארץ),[84] which carried with it horrible discriminatory connotations of excommunication and condemnation.[85] For the Sages, the lack of knowledge (i.e., Talmudic knowledge) was equivalent to the root of all evil. Thus, a person who scorned, disobeyed or simply ignored the Pharisees' traditions would be stigmatized as an ignorant person who was good for nothing.[86]

In contrast, those who carried the prestigious title, "Talmid Chacham" (תלמיד חכם, meaning: a wise disciple of the Talmud), were exalted above the rest and were rewarded with all sorts of benefits. He who hosts a wise disciple in his home and gives him from his assets, it is as if he had brought sacrifices before God.[87] He who gives money to a wise disciple would inherit heaven.[88] A man should sell all he had and marry a daughter of a wise disciple.[89] Wise disciples are exempt from paying taxes.[90] Wise disciples get privileges in the market; they get to sell first, before the rest of the peddlers.[91] All Israel must learn Talmud and those who

---

[84]In the Bible, this term simply means "the people of the land" (see: Gen. 23:12, 42:6; Exo. 5:5; Num. 14:9; 2 Kings 11:14, KJV). But in rabbinic terminology this expression carries an utterly different meaning, of someone who is "completly ignorant" (בור, in Hebrew); see: Weiss, R. (in Hebrew):
רוחמה וייס, אוכלים לדעת: תפקידן התרבותי של הסעודות בספרות חז"ל, בהוצאת הקיבוץ המאוחד, 2010, עמ' 273

[85]b. Talmud, Sotta 22a; Psachim 49b. For further discussion, see: Weiss, R., 294–300.

[86]Rivlin, A. E. (in Hebrew):
ריבלין, א. א., כנגד כולם: פדגוגיה של חז"ל, בהוצאת: ספרית פועלים, רעננה, 1985, עמ' 36–37

[87]b. Talmud, Brachot 10b.

[88]Ibid., Psachim 53b.

[89]Ibid., Psachem 49b.

[90]Ibid., Baba Batra 7b–8a. For farther discussion see: Brodetzky, M. & Wiener, D. H., (in Hebrew):
מודי ברודצקי ודוד הלל וינר, ואם תרצה אמור: חברותא במדרש ובאגדה, הוצאת ראובן מס בע"מ, ירושלים, 2007, עמ' 138

cannot, must support the wise disciples.[92] Moreover, a wise disciple who serves as an expert judge in a Jewish court was exempt from paying fines or being punished for offenses due to his status.[93]

This level of admiration and honour elevated the wise disciple to the highest status in the hierarchy of the Jewish world. By the end of the second century, to be a wise disciple was perceived as a goal in and of itself; as an ideal to which all would aspire. He would become the head and the leader of the community, and he would obtain this prestigious position through nothing other than a phenomenal demonstration of knowledge of the Oral Law.[94]

---

[91]Maimonides, Mishne Torah, Hilchot Talmud Torah, 6.

[92]Rabbi Yosef Karo, Shulchan Aruch, Yore-Dea ,46.

[93]Gruber, 434.

[94]Shalom, G. (in Hebrew):
גרשם שלום, שלושה טיפוסים של יראת שמים יהודית, בתוך: דברים בגו, תל אביב, 1975, עמ' 42–545

Chapter 4

THE RABBIS' NEW COVENANT

The destruction of the Second Temple allowed the rabbis to fully implement their revolutionary reformation.[95] At that stage, the Jewish world had almost no other religious option than to follow the rabbis' Oral Law, almost like a "new covenant." Now, that the traditional, biblical way for atonement was no longer relevant, an alternative had to be made. The Midrash says that one day, Rabbi Yochanan Ben-Zakkai left Jerusalem and Rabbi Joshua was walking behind him, seeing the Temple destroyed, he said: "Woe to us, for the Temple's destruction, where sins were atoned for." So Yochanan replied: "Son, do not be sad, we have a new atonement, which is like it—charity" (גמילות חסדים).[96] The choice had been made; the yeshiva and the Midrash would replace the Temple and the priestly rule as the focal point of Judaism.[97]

[95]Gruber, 213–15.

[96]Avot D'Rabbi Nathan 4:5 (see also: b. Talmud, Brachot 5a).

This gave birth to the rabbis' revolutionary idea of a "new covenant," which no longer required an actual Temple. Instead, the Sages came up with endless ways to atone for sins, and by doing so, they strengthened the dependency of Israel on themselves.[98] Thus, the rabbis taught that anyone who learns the Oral Law, is considered as though he had actually sacrificed a guilt offering.[99] But that was not enough, in order to elevate their status even more, they said:

בזמן שאין בית המקדש קיים, תלמידי חכמים הם כפרה להם לישראל.[100]

Meaning: "While there is no Temple, wise disciples (yeshiva students) are an atonement for Israel." Thus, if the Sinai covenant was based on the blood of the sacrifices,[101] the rabbis' "new covenant" was established upon the rabbis and their traditions. From that moment on, the status of the Written Law began to decline; the Jerusalem Talmud documents Rabbi Haggai's dilemma: "Which is better, the Written Law or the Oral one"? The answer: "According to Exo. 34:27 it is clear that the Oral Law is better than the written one."[102] The Babylonian Talmud took it even further to argue:

לא כרת הקב"ה ברית עם ישראל אלא בשביל דברים שבעל-פה.[103]

---

[97]Shapira-Lavi, A. (in Hebrew):
ענת שפירא לביא, חז"ל עכשיו: מסע בשבילי הסיפור התלמודי, פרדס הוצאה לאור בע"מ, 2017, עמ' 29

[98]Some of the many new rabbinic ways to atone for sins include prayer according to the rabbinic Siddur (b. Talmud, Brachot 32b), learning the Oral Law (Shabbat 30a, Megila 3b), and supporting poor yeshiva students (Midrash Avot D'Rabbi Nathan 4:5).

[99]b. Talmud, Minchot 110a. That was clearly done in defiance against the Sadducees and the Temple.

[100]Midrash Eliyahou Zutta, 2.

[101]According to Exod. 24:8.

[102]Tractate Pea 13b.

Meaning: "God did not make a covenant with Israel, but through the Oral Law". Here we see the Sages new covenant in all its glory and boldness. Of course, this came directly at the expense of the Written Law's validity.[104] This trend continued with yet even a stronger statement:

העוסקין במקרא - מידה ואינה מידה; במשנה - מידה ונוטלין עליה שכר;
בגמרא [תלמוד] – אין לך מידה גדולה מזו.[105]

Meaning: "Those who learn the Written Law gain nothing and lose nothing; those who learn the Mishnah gain something; those who learn the Talmud gain the most." What a staggering statement! Studying the Mishna and the Talmud will grant you favour, but learning the holy of holies—the Bible—will gain you absolutely nothing! Rabbi Eliezer backed this up by saying: "Prevent your children from reason,"[106] which Rashi[107] interpreted: "Do not let them get used to learning the Bible." Accordingly, Maimonides ruled that an educated adult man should not waste his time learning anything apart from the Talmud.[108]

This attitude toward Scriptures led to a situation in which some rabbis were experts in the Oral Law but could not explain verses from the Bible, as in the example of Rabbi Abahu (רבי אבהו) who said: "Rabbi Safra might be an expert

---

[103]Tractate Gittin 60b.

[104]See Roth, M., 127.

[105]b. Talmud, Baba Metzia 33a. For more examples of that trend, see Rivlin, 75.

[106]Ibid., Brachot 28b.

[107]Rabbi Shlomo Yitzchaki (12th hundred AD) is probably the most authoritarian commentator of the Bible and the Talmud in traditional Judaism.

[108]Mishne Torah, Hilchot Talmud Torah 1. For farther discussion see: Lichtenstein, A. (in Hebrew):
אהרן ליכטנשטיין, באור פניך יהלכון: מידות וערכים בעבודת ה', בהוצאת: משכל (ידיעות ספרים), 2012, עמ' 91

in the Oral Law, but he does not know the Bible" (b. Talmud, Avoda Zara 4a).[109] Indeed, the Hebrew Scriptures have lost their relevance compared to the rabbinic "new covenant," and they were now used only as a tool to validate the Oral Law and to strengthen the rabbis' authority.[110] In this case, the end justifies the means, and so the Sages practiced even what they called "biblical castration" (סרס המקרא ודרשהו), in order to extract the meaning they desired from the text.[111]

One time, Rabbi Eliezer interpreted a verse in such a manner, that Rabbi Ishmael thought was too farfetched and distant from the original meaning. He then could not hold himself and rebuked Rabbi Eliezer, saying to him:

הרי אתה אומר לַכָּתוּב: שתוק עד שאדרוש.[112]

Meaning: "But by your interpretation you are telling Scripture, 'Be silent [literally: "shut-up," in Hebrew], and let me interpret.'" Rabbi Eliezer would not retreat from his exaggerated preaching, even if it came at the expense of the plain interpretation of the text. This example reflects a growing and systematic agenda, rather than an exceptional case.[113]

---

[109]Averbach, 282.

[110]See Elior, 132–34; and Gruber, 149–50.

[111]According to b. Talmud, Baba Batra 119b. see Piekarz, M. (in Hebrew):
מנדל פייקאז', חסידות פולין: מגמות רעיוניות בין שתי המלחמות ובגזרות ת"ש-תש"ה (ה'שואה'), בהוצאת: מוסד ביאליק, ירושלים, 1990, עמ' 178
and also: Gamliel, C. (in Hebrew):
חנוך גמליאל, רש"י כפרשן וכבלשן: תפיסות תחביריות בפירוש רש"י לתורה, בהוצאת: מוסד ביאליק, ירושלים, 2010, עמ' 176–170

[112]Navon, 41.

[113]See Wise, H., in: Lipsker, A. & Kushelevsky, R. (eds.), in Hebrew:
הלל ויס, בתוך: אבידב ליפסקר ורלה קושלבסקי (עורכים), מעשה סיפור - מחקרים בסיפורת היהודית, הוצאת אוניברסיטת בר אילן, 2006, עמ' 390–391

Another device, or method, which was made extremely popular by the Sages, was the practice of building fences around the Torah (לעשות סייג לתורה), to make sure that the laws would not be broken.[114] Gradually, these fences led to the creation of countless oral regulations, beyond the six hundred and thirteen commandments of the Written Law.[115]

An example of this method can be clearly seen in the so called "kosher" laws of meat and dairy (based on Exod. 23:19, 34:26; Deut. 14:21). In the entire Bible there is no commandment which prohibits eating meat and dairy together. Bible scholars argue that the three times when the Torah prohibits cooking a kid-goat in his mother's milk have nothing to do with the rabbinic kosher laws. Instead, they deal with God forbidding Israel to practice pagan rituals of worship by cooking goats in their own milk.[116] In fact, even Maimonides admitted that this is the authentic biblical reason.[117] The Bible itself presents examples of key figures who ate meat and dairy with no consciousness of guilt (e.g., Abraham – Gen 18:8; King David – 2 Sam 17:29).

Today, however, thanks to this rabbinic practice of building fences, there are hundreds of binding kosher laws that are nowhere to be found in the Torah. Again, supposedly basing

---

[114]Mishnah, Avot 1:1. Actually, Rabbi Akiva admitted that the rabbis' tradition is a fence around the Torah (3:16).

[115]One of the verses that the Sages used in order to justify making endless fences to the law, was Lev. 18:30. The B. Talmud, Yevamot 21a and Moed-Katan 5a, say: "therefore shall ye keep mine ordinance"– make ordinance for my ordinance. In Hebrew: ושמרתם את משמרתי - עשו משמרת למשמרתי

[116]See: Ginsberg, H. (in Hebrew):
חיים גינזברג, כתבי אוגרית, הוצאת מוסד ביאליק, 1936, עמ' 77–79
And also: Cassuto, M. (in Hebrew):
מ. ד. קאסוטו, האלה ענת: שירי עלילה כנעניים בתקופת האבות, הוצאת מוסד ביאליק, 1950, עמ' 9, 40

[117]In his book, *The Guide for the Perplexed*, in Hebrew: מורה נבוכים לרמב"ם, חלק ג' פרק מ"ח

their innovations on the Bible itself, the rabbis had the freedom to say that they did not invent anything new, rather, they had received everything from their forefathers.[118] Thus, when they wanted to compliment a certain rabbi, they would say that he never uttered anything he did not hear from his rabbi.[119]

From that point forward, they argued that each generation is worse than the previous one.[120] Their educational assumption was that the past was better than the future, and therefore, it was permissible to clarify, expand, and interpret the Mishna, but it was absolutely forbidden to undermine it.[121] Thus, tradition became the most dominant factor in the existence of the Pharisaic religion, and keeping that tradition was the key to establishing its authoritative nature, to impose it on Israel, and to sustain it through the ages.[122] Of course, the advent of rabbinic Judaism and the centrality of the yeshiva were absolutely essential, enabling the rabbis to implement their ideas and to govern all spheres of life with maximum efficiency.[123]

---

[118]b. Talmud, Megila 10b.

[119]Ibid., Sukkah 27b.

[120]Ibid., Sanhedrin 98a; Shabbat 112b.

[121]Rivlin, 35.

[122]Ibid., 35, 129–131.

[123]Ibid., 48. See also Breuer, M., in: Grossman, A. & Kaplan, J. (eds.), in Hebrew:
מרדכי ברויאר, בתוך: אברהם גרוסמן ויוסף קפלן (עורכים), קהל ישראל: השלטון העצמי היהודי לדורותיו - ימי הביניים והעת החדשה המוקדמת (כרך ב), בהוצאת: מרכז זלמן שזר לחקר תולדות העם היהודי, ירושלים, 2004, עמ' 243–47.

Chapter 5

THE PHILOSOPHY BEHIND STUDYING THE ORAL LAW

The close ties which the Pharisees had with the Greco-Roman world caused them to adopt many of their beliefs and customs, such as witchcraft and other superstitious rituals which were completely alien to Scripture. The Sages who faced this reality tried sometimes to legitimize these pagan patterns and even convert them into their idea of Judaism.[124] This chapter and the next will deal with foreign philosophies and beliefs which penetrated the rabbinic religion. This chapter will focus mainly on the Greek philosophical influence on four essential aspects of rabbinic Judaism and the Oral Law.

A. **Philosophers as Rulers:** The wise disciple (תלמיד-חכם) stood at the very top of the hierarchy of the Jewish world. Their deep knowledge of the Oral Law gave them authority to govern the community.[125] In other words, the most essential criterion by which a man could judge and rule was the measure of wisdom he manifested concerning the Talmud.

---

[124]Lieberman, S. (in Hebrew):
שאול ליברמן, יוונים ויוונות בארץ ישראל, בהוצאת מוסד ביאליק, ירושלים, 1962 עמ' 73-74

[125]Shalom, 544.

The rabbinic utopia is probably the only contemporary society which puts the intellectuals (i.e., philosopher) at the top of the pyramid. The closest existing model would be Plato's ideal philosophical government.[126] No wonder then that the members of the Sanhedrin, as Rabbi Yochanan Ben-Zakkai for example,[127] had to be knowledgeable in all wisdom, including the wisdom of the Greeks.[128] Maimonides considered himself a disciple of Aristotle,[129] saw Moses as the chief philosopher, and even referred to [rabbinic] Judaism as a philosophical religion.[130]

B. Philosophical Methods of Learning the Oral Law:

Rabbinic law and, in fact, the whole literature of the Sages, was influenced by Plato and Aristotelian philosophy, and therefore it is not surprising that the studies in yeshiva are characterized by its endless contradictions and multiple arguments.[131] The most important and influential encounter between rabbinical Judaism and Greek philosophy probably took place in Alexandria, which prepared the ground for the wisdom of the future sages.[132]

---

[126]Brown, B., interviewed in "Israel Hayom" (ישראל היום), weekend edition, 29.09.17, 28.

[127]See, b. Talmud, Sukkah 28a; and also: Wiesel, 53.

[128]Harari, Y., The Sages and the Occult, in: Schwartz, J., Tomson, P. J., Safrai, S. & Safrai, Z. (eds.), The Literature of the Sages, Second Part, Fortress Press, 2007, 521–64.

[129]Mankin, B., in: Ravitzky, A. (ed.), in Hebrew:
מנקין, ב., בתוך: אביעזר רביצקי (עורך), הרמב"ם: שמרנות, מקוריות, מהפכנות - הגות וחדשנות (כרך ב), בהוצאת: מרכז זלמן שזר לחקר תולדות העם היהודי, ירושלים, 2009, עמ' 311

[130]Ibid., 551.

[131]Even-Chen, A. (in Hebrew):
אבן-חן, א., עקדת יצחק: בפרשנות המיסטית והפילוסופית של המקרא, בהוצאת: משכל (ידיעות ספרים), 2006, עמ' 55

The Talmud's method "Shakla v'Tatria" (שקלא וטריא)[133] operates on the premise that the search for truth is never a monologue and is not carried out by an argument aimed at deciding. Instead of achieving agreement, the goal of casuistry is to expand knowledge by the multiplicity of possibilities.[134] This method is remarkably similar to the Scholastic philosophy,[135] which deals with both casuistry and an abstract dialectic negotiation.[136]

Accordingly, the Babylonian Talmud (Sotah 49b; Baba Kama 83a) reports that Rabbi Shimon's school accommodated 1,500 students, five hundred of whom studied Greek wisdom.[137] The typical yeshiva is known for its heated debates about Law, Midrash, and more. In fact, some argue that the entire Mishnah is one great display of debates.[138]

---

[132] Schweid, E. (in Hebrew):
שביד, א., הפילוסופים הגדולים שלנו: הפילוסופיה היהודית בימי הביניים, בהוצאת: משכל (ידיעות ספרים), 2009, עמ' 12

[133] This principle of learning means: give and take, as a style of intellectual dialectic-negotiation. See Calderon, R., in: Aloni, N. (ed.), in Hebrew:
קלדרון, ר., בתוך: נמרוד אלוני (עורך), דיאלוגים מעצימים בחינוך ההומניסטי, בהוצאת: הקיבוץ המאוחד, רעננה, 2008, עמ' 122

[134] Greenberg, S. (in Hebrew):
סטיבן גרינברג, עם אלוהים ועם אנשים: הומוסקסואליות במסורת היהודית, בהוצאת: הקיבוץ המאוחד, רעננה, 2013, עמ' 205

[135] The Scholastic philosophy was an educational tradition and method of thought that had been developed in early mid-evil times; in its base stands a philosophical-theological strive to search for divine truth by means of intellectual and systemic understanding. Taken from the Hebrew Encyclopaedia (in Hebrew):
יהושע פראוור, (עורך ראשי), האנציקלופדיה העברית, כרך עשרים וחמישה, חברה להוצאת אנציקלופדיות בע"מ, 1974, עמ' 996

[136] Avineri, S., in: Weinstein, J. (ed.), in Hebrew:
אבינרי ש., בתוך: יהושע ויינשטיין (עורך), אי-ציות ודמוקרטיה, הוצאת שלם, ירושלים, 1998, עמ' 167
See also in: Friedlander, Y., (in Hebrew):
יהודה פרידלנדר, בין הלכה להשכלה: מקומן של סוגיות הלכתיות במרקם סוגות ספרותיות, בהוצאת אוניברסיטת בר אילן, 2004, עמ' 20

[137] Averbach, 28.

[138] Neuwirth, R. (in Hebrew):
רונן נויבירט, לגעת בזמן: החגים כחוויה בעולם המדרש, בהוצאת: משכל (ידיעות ספרים), 2016, עמ' 152

C. Thirteen Characteristics of Learning: The rabbis claim that the thirteen methods by which they interpreted Torah[139] were given to Moses at Sinai.[140] The problem with this claim is that these methods are found in the Hellenistic world. In fact, all thirteen are a duplication of the terminology used by the Greek philosophers and poets for their classical literature, written many generations after Moses and before the time of the Sages. Rabbi Hillel seems to have established the systematic interpretation of the Bible, relying on known Greek patterns.[141] This led some contemporary scholars of Talmud and Halakah to refer to the influence of Greek-Aristotelian logic on the rabbinic interpretation methods as an absolute fact.[142]

D. Greek Academia in the Talmudic Yeshiva: Everything mentioned above, the rabbis' rule in accordance with the Platonic model of the utopian state, governed by philosophers,[143] the methods of learning, which is identical to Greek Philosophy. patterns of intellectual investigation, plus the fact that the rabbis urged the study of the Talmud for its own sake (תלמוד תורה לשמה), as a philosophical and moral

---

[139]In Hebrew: י"ג המידות שהתורה נדרשת בהן

[140]See Shapira, J. (in Hebrew):
יוסף שפירא, הגות, הלכה וציונות: על עולמו הרוחני של הרב יצחק יעקב ריינס, בהוצאת הקיבוץ המאוחד, רעננה, 2002, עמ' 257

[141]Levin, I. L., in: Barkai, G. & Shiller, E. (eds.), 160–62.

[142]Ravitsky, A., in: Rosenak, A. (ed.), in Hebrew:
רביצקי, א., בתוך: אבינועם רוזנק (עורך), הלכה, מטה-הלכה ופילוסופיה: עיון רב-תחומי, בהוצאת מאגנס, האוניברסיטה העברית, ירושלים, 2011, עמ' 242

[143]For similarities between Plato's dialogs and Talmudic discourse, see: Howland, J., Plato and the Talmud, Cambridge University Press, 2010.

> concept,[144] and as an obligation which carried no other intention than the act itself[145]—all these were done in the context of the yeshiva.

According to the Written Law, the objective of learning the Law was in order to act according to it. Every time the command, "learn" (ללמוד), or, "keep" (לשמור), appears in relation to the Law, the command, "do" (לעשות), appears alongside it in the very same context.[146] Thus Moses emphasizes the need to learn, to keep, and to do the Laws of the Torah, but he never promoted studying it only for the sake of studying, as the Sages teach. Moreover, rabbinic tradition has turned the act of learning Talmud into work itself (תורתו אמנותו)—a never-ending occupation which bestows merit, both in this world and in the world to come.[147]

Of course, this "work" took place in the yeshiva, which (as shown above) was a duplication of the Greek academy.[148] Disciples were to spend all their time studying Talmud out of similar motivation, learning through similar methods, and sometimes even reciting the same statements, as their fellow philosophers.[149]

---

[144]Rivlin, A. E., 24.

[145]Breuer, M. (in Hebrew): מרדכי ברויאר, פרקי מקראות, בהוצאת תבונות, 2009, עמ' 348-349

[146]E.g. Due 4:1, 6–5, 10–14, 5:1, 29–32, 6:1; 11:19–22, 17:19, 31:12.

[147]Midrash Pele-Yoetz, chapter Halacha, 184, see also 222.

[148]More about the similarities between the Academia and the yeshiva, see Oz Almog interview in "Israel Hayom" (ישראל היום) newspaper, 15.02.13.

[149]For examples see: Halevi, E. (in Hebrew):
אלימלך הלוי, האגדה ההסטורית-ביוגרפית, לאור מקורות יווניים ולאטיניים, תל אביב, 1975

Chapter 6

THE PAGAN ROOTS OF THE RABBINIC CUSTOMS

The previous chapter dealt with the philosophical rabbinic features, which were deeply rooted in the Greek mindset. This chapter examines the pagan roots of only five (out of many more) important practices of rabbinic Judaism.

A. Repetition of Mantras

A mantra is defined as an expression of syllables, words, and sentences spoken in the form of ongoing repetition, in the belief that this action releases spiritual powers. Apparently, the source of the mantras was Hinduism and was originally made in the Sanskrit language.[150] Today, many religions have elements of mantras that are used as part of regular prayers.

Rabbinic Judaism is filled with special mantras which are used as good luck charms. For example: In order to find something that has been lost, one can chant the name of Rabbi Meir three times.[151] One could chant certain prescribed verses from the Psalms in order to escape any trouble.[152] Saying verses that

[150]Rosenthal, R. (in Hebrew):
רוביק רוזנטל, הלקסיקון של החיים: שפות במרחב הישראלי, בהוצאת: כתר ספרים בע"מ, 2007, עמ' 127

[151]According to b. Talmud, Avodah Zarah 18a.

begin and end with the letter, *nun*, provides protection from the evil eye, evil speech (e.g., gossip), and witchcraft.[153] Screaming, "Amen," from the top of your lungs will get you to heaven.[154]

In fact, research on biblical prayer, compared to "rabbinic prayer," has suggested that praying out of the Siddur (i.e., the rabbinical prayer book) is closer to chanting mantras than to prayer as found in the Tanakh. The Siddur was composed by the Sages, beginning in the Second Century and was finalized toward the end of the first millennium. In contrast to the personal and spontaneous nature of biblical prayer, the rabbinic style of prayer has a fixed text for each and every event.[155]

Also, "praying" from the Siddur must be done in a specific place (i.e., the synagogue),[156] at particular times (morning, noon, and evening),[157] and with a certain kind of people and not others (i.e., no women)[158]—all determined by the rabbis. Indeed, the rabbis have decreed when to pray, how to pray, where to pray, and with whom to pray. But in complete contrast, biblical (Old Testament) prayer is individual, never repetitious, and is never restricted to one place or from anyone.

---

[152]In the book, "Avodat H'Kodesh" (עבודת הקודש), by Rabbi Chaim Yosef David Azulai (known as the "Chida"), who was a Kabbalist and halachic authority, born in Jerusalem in the 18th century.

[153]Ibid. The verses are: Gen 18:15; Lev 13:9; Numb 32:32; Jer 50:8; Ps 46:5; 71:21; 78:12; Prov 7:17; 20:27; Song 4:11; and 1 Chron 12:2.

[171]b. Talmud, Shabbat 119b.
154

[155]Goren, Zechariah & Dror, Miriam (in Hebrew):
זכריה גורן ומרים דרור, על סידור התפילה (מדריך דידקטי), מכון מופ"ת, רעננה, 2000, עמ' 47

[156]b. Talmud, Brachot 6a.

[157]Replacing the times of sacrifices offering made by the priests. See in: Midrash Avot D'Rabbi Nathan (אבות דרבי נתן) 4:5.

[158]b. Talmud, Brachot 6b

B. Belief in Astrology and Luck: The dependence on astrology and its worship typified the customs of many pagans, such as the Babylonians in Mesopotamia and the ancient Egyptians.[159] The ties between the Sages in Israel and the Gentiles, led them to believe in astrology, witchcraft, and other superstitions that are completely alien to the Bible.[160]

Although its sources lie in the Babylonian religion, the belief in astrology found favor in broad rabbinic circles in the Second Temple Period.[161] In fact, many rabbis demonstrated extensive knowledge of the doctrine of astrology, despite the association it had with pagan beliefs. Some of the Sages even considered themselves experts in that field.[162]

An example of this can be seen in the words of Rabbi Papa,[163] who advised not to go to court against Gentiles in certain Hebrew months because of bad luck.[164] In another place, the Talmud gives an astrological prognosis of a man's future according to his specific date of birth.[165] Moreover,

---

[159]Mazar, B. (ed.), Biblical Encyclopedia (in Hebrew):
בנימין מזר (עורך), אנציקלופדיה מקראית: אוצר הידיעות של המקרא ותקופתו - ד: כבד – מלתחה, בהוצאת: מוסד ביאליק, ירושלים, 1962, עמ' 47

[160]Lieberman.

[161]Orbach, 245.

[162]Harari.

[163]A famous rabbi who lived in Babylon and served as chief of a yeshiva.

[164]Gafni, I. (in Hebrew):
ישעיהו גפני, יהודי בבל בתקופת התלמוד: חיי החברה והרוח, בהוצאת: מרכז זלמן שזר לחקר תולדות העם היהודי, ירושלים, 1990, עמ' 167

[165]b.Talmud, Shabbat 156a. translated from Aramaic by: Bialik, H. & Ravitzky, I. (in Hebrew):
ביאליק, ח. ורבניצקי, י., ספר האגדה, הוצאת דביר, תל-אביב, 1962, עמ' 620

archeological research has found mosaic zodiac[166] figures in the floors of certain synagogues dating back to the times of the Mishna. In fact, ancient rabbinic literature reveals a rather positive attitude of some Sages towards the zodiac; not only that they did not protest against this phenomenon, some even encouraged the placing of the zodiac in synagogues.[167]

C. **The Mezuzah as a Good Luck Charm:** The command to attach a mezuzah to the doorpost, as manifested in rabbinic tradition, is never explicitly mentioned in the Torah.[168] The biblical meaning of the phrase "mezuzah" simply refers to the doorpost which frames the entrance to a house, a room, etc.[169]

If the rabbinical interpretation was valid, then Judges 16:3 will make no religious sense whatsoever: "But Samson lay till midnight, and at midnight he arose and took hold of the doors of the gate of the city and the two posts, and pulled them up, bar and all, and put them on his shoulders and carried them to the top of the hill that is in front of Hebron". The Hebrew word for the phrase "posts" is literally "mezuzot" (הַמְּזוּזוֹת). Should it be understood, according to that verse, that the gentile Philistines had two mezuzahs on their doorpost? Of course not! Samson simply pulled up the gates of the city, grabbing them by the doorposts.

---

[166]The zodiac represents a pagan belief in the horoscopic control which the stars in the sky poses over everything that happens in the earth (see: Zanger, W., Jewish Worship, Pagan Symbols, published by: Ancient Israel, Biblical Archaeology Society, Aug. 24, 2012).

[167]Zanger. See also: Aharon Oppenheimer, Rabbi Judah ha-Nasi (in Hebrew):
אהרון אופנהיימר, רבי יהודה הנשיא, בהוצאת: מרכז זלמן שזר לחקר תולדות העם היהודי, ירושלים, 2007, עמ' 13

[168]Mazar, 781.

[169] See the Biblical Hebrew Dictionary, by Kadari, M. (in Hebrew):
קדרי, מ. צ., מילון העברית המקראית, בהוצאת אוניברסיטת בר-אילן, רמת גן, 2007, עמ' 595

Moreover, in the entire Bible there is not a single mention of any instruction concerning the way by which the alleged laws of the mezuzah must be implemented; Deuteronomy 22:8 reads: "When you build a new house, you shall make a parapet for your roof, that you may not bring the guilt of blood upon your house, if anyone should fall from it". If the commandment to put a mezuzah was as important as the rabbis' claim,[170] how come there is no mention of it here? Could the mezuzah be less important than the parapet?!

Hence, it is interesting to investigate how the mezuzah was turned onto an amulet which can guard the house against evil.[171] Historical and archeological research found that pagan nations from Mesopotamia used to mark their entries with different kinds of "mezuzahs", which carried symbols of idols. Amulets of this kind were also found in Egypt, where this practice was made in order to keep the inhabitants of the home from all sorts of evil.[172]

The rabbis expanded the concept of the mezuzah into a ritual amulet that included passages from the Torah, written on a special parchment. Also, they determined who needs a mezuzah, what should be written in the mezuzah, how should it be written, exactly where to attach the mezuzah, how to

[170] See these rabbinic sources for example (in Hebrew):
קיצור שולחן ; ילקוט שמעוני שמות, פרשת בא; מדרש "שכל טוב" פרשת בא, פרק י"ב
ערוך" סימן י"א, הלכות מזוזה א

[171]The j. Talmud record Rabbi Judah the Prince (יהודה הנשיא) gives a certain king a special mezuzah as a gift which shall protect his home. See: Tigay, J. H. (in Hebrew):
יעקב חיים טיגאי, מקרא לישראל: פירוש מדעי למקרא - מקרא לישראל: דברים - כרך ראשון א, א – טז, יז, בהוצאת:
האוניברסיטה העברית בירושלים, עם עובד י"ל מאגנס, 2016, עמ' 280

[172]Mazar, 780–82.

hang it, how to maintain it, etc.[173] In fact, attaching the mezuzah on the exact right location of the doorpost is considered by the rabbis to impact the chances for good luck.[174] Also, the mezuzah must be checked every few years by an authorized expert in order to determine if it is still kosher (i.e., in good condition).[175] Of course, this service includes a monetary payment and does not come for free.

Thus, by turning this good luck charm into a whole set of new rules and regulations, the Sages used it as another tool by which they could have control and authority over the people of Israel. Interestingly enough, some rabbis today admit that this practice is nothing other than the inheritance of an old pagan ritual; a form of amulet that originated in a pagan practice.[176]

D. **Using the Tefillin as an Amulet:** Biblical scholars and even some of the most prominent rabbinic commentators agree that Deuteronomy 6:8 has nothing to do with the tefillin (phylacteries), and should only be understood symbolically.[177] Bible research indicates

---

[173]See Maimonides, Mishneh Torah, Hilchot Mezuzah 5.

[174]See example in: Yoram Bilu, With Us More than Ever Before – Making the Absent Rebbe Present in Messianic Chabad (in Hebrew):

יורם בילו, אתנו יותר מתמיד: הנכחת הרבי בחב"ד המשיחית, האוניברסיטה הפתוחה, רעננה, 2017, 81

[175]See Maimonides, Mishneh Torah, Hilchot Mezuzah 5:9. And also: Dov Schwartz, Contradiction and Concealment in Medieval Jewish Thought (in Hebrew):
דב שוורץ, סתירה והסתרה בהגות היהודית בימי הביניים, הוצאת אוניברסיטת בר אילן, 2002, 243

[176]Marx, D., in: Rosenak, A. (ed.), in Hebrew:
אבינועם רוזנק (עורך), היהדות הרפורמית: הגות, תרבות וחברה, בהוצאת: מכון ון ליר בירושלים, הקיבוץ המאוחד, 2014, עמ' 344

[177]See: Schorr, J. H. (ed.), in Hebrew:
יהושע השיל שור (עורך), יהושוע השיל שור: מאמרים, בהוצאת: מוסד ביאליק, ירושלים, 1972, עמ' 193
And: Mazar, B. (ed.), In Hebrew:
בנימין מזר (עורך), אנציקלופדיה מקראית: אוצר הידיעות של המקרא ותקופתו - ח: שם – תתני, בהוצאת: מוסד ביאליק, ירושלים, 1982, עמ' 893

that until the end of the Second Temple era, Deuteronomy 6:8 was perceived only in an allegoric and symbolic manner. [178] In fact, a close investigation of the Hebrew in Exodus 13:9, 16 reveals a fascinating parallelization between the phrase "Zikaron" (memorial) to the phrase "Totafot" (frontlets):

Exodus 13:9: וְהָיָה לְךָ לְאוֹת עַל־יָדְךָ **וּלְזִכָּרוֹן** בֵּין עֵינֶיךָ

"And it shall be to you as a sign on your hand and as a **memorial** between your eyes".

Exodus 13:16: וְהָיָה לְאוֹת עַל־יָדְכָה **וּלְטוֹטָפֹת** בֵּין עֵינֶיךָ

"It shall be as a mark on your hand or **frontlets** between your eyes".

The Hebrew here makes it clear that the Biblical interpretation of the phrase "frontlets" (טוֹטָפֹת) must be understood as a synonym to the phrase "memorial" (זִכָּרוֹן), and has nothing to do with the rabbinic commandment of putting-on the Tefillin.

Nevertheless, the tefillin has become one of the most prominent and important symbols of rabbinic law and tradition (for example, according to Babylonian Talmud Kiddushin 35a).

However, is it based on Moses' Torah or on something else? There is solid evidence that the practice of putting on certain variations of tefillin was common among the Jewish people, long before the era of the Pharisees. In fact, amulets similar to

---

And: Elitzur, Y. (in Hebrew)
יהודה אליצור, ישראל והמקרא: מחקרים גיאוגרפיים, היסטוריים והגותיים, הוצאת
אוניברסיטת בר אילן, 2000, עמ' 16
And also: Shalom, Sharon. From Sinai to Ethiopia (in Hebrew):
שרון שלום, מסיני לאתיופיה: עולמה ההלכתי והרעיוני של יהדות אתיופיה, בהוצאת: משכל (ידיעות ספרים), 2012, עמ' 363,
הערת שוליים מס' 168

[178] Mazar, 893.

the tefillin were commonly adopted from ancient cultures of idol worshipers, especially in the Mediterranean area.[179]

The tefillin were perceived as magical figurative symbols, and the use of such amulets, attached to the head or arms, were practiced in the ancient world by pagans, long before the first century.[180] Furthermore, holy writings attached to the body and portrayed as amulets were used by various pagan peoples. For example, an amulet which resembles tefillin was discovered in Mesopotamia. This particular amulet had a brief inscription, dedicated to an ancient idol. In fact, other ancient religions also used to insert holy writings into amulets and connect them to the body, just like the tefillin.[181]

Toward the end of the Second Temple Period, the admiration of tefillin among the Jewish people was already widespread, and there are testimonies in rabbinical literature that the Sages themselves believed in the mystical power of the tefillin as a good luck charm, used for guarding and protection against the evil-eye and all sorts of bad fortunes.[182]

In the Talmud we see that tefillin and amulets were closely related.[183] The tefillin and the amulets were often mentioned together, as synonymous expressions, and the adoration of the tefillin as good luck charms was actually made most popular during the Talmudic period. The Sages have considered the

---

[179]Mazar, 886–88.

[180]Haran, M. (in Hebrew):
מנחם הרן, האסופה המקראית: תהליכי הגיבוש עד סוף ימי בית שני ושינויי הצורה עד מוצאי ימי הביניים - חלק ב, בהוצאת:
מוסד ביאליק, האוניברסיטה העברית בירושלים, י"ל מאגנס, 2003, עמ' 180

[181]Mazar, 886.

[182]E.g., b. Talmud, Brachot 23a.

[183]Ibid., Avoda Zara 39a.

tefillin as amulets of divine power which could protect men. Their final shape and form, as was determined by the rabbis, is clearly taken from ancient Egypt, where a figure of a sacred snake was tied to the head as a good luck charm, and this resembles the traditional tefillin.[184] Ever since, the practice of wearing the tefillin has become more important, and the rabbis have transformed it into a binding practice which is accompanied by specific laws.[185]

E. **Prostration over Tombs of Saints:** The origin of this ritual, which surrounds sacred tombs and involves worshiping the dead, is rooted deeply in the customs of ancient pagan peoples.[186] In fact, the practice of prostration on tombs of "saints" was widespread among so-called Christian sects before it was adopted by the rabbis. These practices usually included rituals where candles were thrown into the fire as symbols of their superstitions beliefs.[187]

These customs were adopted by the Sages and are recorded in the Talmud.[188] The practice of prostration is not unique

---

[184]Tur-Sinai, N. H. (in Hebrew):
נ.ה. טור-סיני, הלשון והספר: בעיות יסוד במדע הלשון ובמקורותיה הספרותיים - כרך האמונות והדעות, בהוצאת: מוסד ביאליק, ירושלים, 1955, עמ' 127

[185]Mazar, 885–89.

[186]Rappel, Y. (in Hebrew):
יואל רפל, מועדי ישראל: אנציקלופדיה שימושית לשבת ולחג - למעיין, לסטודנט, לתלמיד, בהוצאת: משרד הביטחון, רעננה, 1990, עמ' 448
See also: Mazar, B. (in Hebrew):
בנימין מזר (עורך), אנציקלופדיה מקראית: אוצר הידיעות של המקרא ותקופתו - ד: כבד – מלתחה, מוסד ביאליק, ירושלים, 1962, עמ' 759-760

[187]Rappel, 206; see also: Mushon, G. (in Hebrew):
מושון גבאי (עורך), מדריך ישראל החדש: אנציקלופדיה, מסלולי טיול - כרך 3: הגליל העליון וחופו, כתר הוצאה לאור, ידיעות אחרונות, משרד הביטחון, 2001, עמ' 277
And also: Bilu, Y. (in Hebrew):
יורם בילו, שושביני הקדושים: חולמים, מרפאות וצדיקים בספר העירוני בישראל, הוצאת הספרים של אוניברסיטת חיפה, 2005, עמ' 34-35

to rabbinic religion. It is most prevalent among Muslims, "Christians," and other religions, and there are clear parallels between the celebration around the graves of Muslim saints and the rabbinic prostration customs.[189]

Today there are close to two hundred recorded sites of rabbinic saints in Israel,[190] which attract millions of pilgrims each year and are even financially supported by the government.[191] Of course, these gravesites only strengthen the dependency under which the rabbis are keeping their followers, and also provide an enormous source of revenue for rabbinic organizations.[192]

This paper is too limited to explore all the other pagan beliefs which have found a home in rabbinical Judaism, such as the existence of demons in bathrooms,[193] the breaking of glass in weddings,[194] reincarnation of souls,[195] belief in the existence of the little Mermaid,[196] practices of

---

[188]E.g., b. Talmud, Ta'anit 16a; Sotah 34b; see also: Shtal, A., in: Barkai, G. & Shiller, E. (eds.), in Hebrew:
אברהם שטאל, בתוך: אלי שילר (עורך), אריאל: כתב עת לידיעת ארץ ישראל - דת ופולחן וקברי קדושים מוסלמים בארץ-ישראל, הוצאת ספרים אריאל, ירושלים, 1996, עמ' 14

[189]Bilu, 29, 33.

[190]See Michelson, M., Milner, M. & Salomon, Y. (in Hebrew):
מנחם מיכלסון, יהודה סלומון ומשה מילנר, מקומות קדושים וקברי צדיקים בארץ ישראל, בהוצאת: משרד הביטחון, 2000, עמ' 11

[191] See Schlesinger, Y. article, published in Israel Hayom (ישראל היום) newspaper, 11.10.17., 30–35.

[192]Michelson, M., Milner, M. & Salomon, Y., 11–12.

[193]Dagan, H. (in Hebrew):
חגי דגן, המיתולוגיה היהודית, בהוצאת: מפה – מיפוי והוצאה לאור, 2003, עמ' 81

[194]See Alon Levkovitz, How Are Halloween & A Jewish Wedding Ceremony Connected?, 2013.

[195]Yagel, A. B. H. (in Hebrew):
אברהם בן חנניה יגל, ספר גיא חזיון, בהוצאת: מרכז זלמן שזר לחקר תולדות העם היהודי, ירושלים, 1997, עמ' 104

[196]Mazar, B (in Hebrew):
בנימין מזר (עורך), אנציקלופדיה מקראית: אוצר הידיעות של המקרא ותקופתו - ח: שם – תתני, בהוצאת: מוסד ביאליק, ירושלים, 1982, עמ' 520
And also: Mendelson, H. & Yom-Tov, Y (eds.), in Hebrew):

witchcraft,[197] God versus the god of the sea,[198] the belief in a time of purgatory,[199] prayers for raising the souls of the dead ("kaddish"),[200] the industry of amulets,[201] turning Purim into a pagan carnival,[202] putting rocks on tombstones,[203] worshipping pictures of saints,[204] using sacred candles,[205] changing the new year (i.e., Rosh Hashanah) into a pagan date,[206] and the custom of women separating a tenth of the challah bread (הפרשת חלה).[207]

The pagan roots of many of the rabbinic traditions further weakens the alleged connection between the Oral Law and the spirit of the Bible. But in spite of this, the next chapter

---

היינריך מנדלסון ויורם יום טוב (עורכים), החי והצומח של ארץ-ישראל: אנציקלופדיה שימושית מאויירת - כרך 7 – יונקים, בהוצאת: משרד הביטחון, רעננה, 1988, עמ' 240

[197]Beitner, 329. See also: Bazak, J. (in Hebrew):
יעקב בזק, הלכות כשפים והלכות נטיעת קשואים, אוניברסיטת בר-אילן, ו', 1968, עמ' 156-166

[198]b. Talmud, Baba Batra 74b.

[199]Benjamin Lau (in Hebrew):
בנימין לאו, חכמים - כרך שלישי: ימי גליל, בהוצאת: משכל (ידיעות ספרים), 2008, עמ' 141
See also: Elon, A. (in Hebrew): ארי אלון, עלמא די, בהוצאת: משכל (ידיעות ספרים), 2011, עמ' 147

[200]Eran Kimchi (in Hebrew):
ערן קמחי, שחרור המקום: דרך למהגר בעולם, בהוצאת: פרדס הוצאה לאור בע"מ, 2016, עמ' 123-124

[201]Gabriel Barkai & Eli Shiller (Eds.), in Hebrew:
גבריאל ברקאי ואלי שילר (עורכים), אריאל: כתב עת לידיעת ארץ ישראל - קמיעות ברפואה העממית בקרב הבדווים בנגב, הוצאת ספרים אריאל, 2006, עמ' 6-7

[202]Bar-Navi, E. (ed.), in Hebrew:
אלי בר-נביא (עורך), האטלס ההיסטורי של תולדות עם ישראל, בהוצאת ידיעות אחרונות, ספרי חמד, 1993: 72

[203]Amots, D. (in Hebrew):
אמוץ דפני, עצים מקודשים בישראל, בהוצאת: הקיבוץ המאוחד, רעננה, 2010, עמ' 104-105

[204]Pelli, M (in Hebrew):
משה פלאי, עטרה ליושנה: המאבק ליצירת יהדות ההשכלה, בהוצאת: הקיבוץ המאוחד, רעננה, 2012, עמ' 66-67

[205]Ibid., 66, 182; see also: Shiller, E, in: Barkai, G. & Shiller, E. (eds.), in Hebrew:
אלי שילר, בתוך: גדעון ביגר ואלי שילר (עורכים), אריאל : כתב עת לידיעת ארץ ישראל - אתרים ומקומות בארץ-ישראל, הוצאת ספרים אריאל, 1988, עמ' 96

[206]Licht, J. S. (ed.), in Hebrew:
יעקוב שלום ליכט, (עורך), מועדי ישראל: זמנים ומועדים בתקופת המקרא ובימי בית שני, בהוצאת: מוסד ביאליק, ירושלים, 1988, עמ' 108

[207]El-Or, T. (in Hebrew):
תמר אלאור, מקומות שמורים: מגדר ואתניות במחוזות הדת והתשובה, בהוצאת: עם עובד, רעננה, 2006, עמ' 58-61

will show how the Sages tried—artificially and with much interpretive manipulation—to connect the Oral Law back to the Tanakh, even if it meant twisting the plain meaning of the text and changing entire words.

Chapter 7

THE ORAL LAW AND THE OLD TESTAMENT

The absolute absence of justification for the Oral Law in the Tanakh has caused the rabbis to take radical measures in order to justify its authority. The Bible's divine status meant that the Sages would have to plant themselves and the Oral Law within the text.[208] This chapter will present a dozen examples of how they attempted to find biblical justification for the alleged Oral Law.

1. Exodus 34:27 says that God told Moses to write (כְּתָב־לְךָ) these words, for in accordance (עַל־פִּי) with these words, He is going to make a covenant with Israel. Verse 28 says: "and He wrote (וַיִּכְתֹּב) upon the tables the words…" (KJV). The Hebrew phrase עַל־פִּי (according to) in this context can only mean that this covenant was made "according to" the written words.[209] Nevertheless, the Babylonian Talmud ignored the obvious and argued,

[208] Gruber, 101, 149–58.

[209] See the Biblical Hebrew Dictionary, by Kadari, M. (in Hebrew):
קדרי, מ. צ., מילון העברית המקראית, בהוצאת אוניברסיטת בר-אילן, רמת גן, 2007, עמ' 799, 848

based on this verse, that the covenant was made orally (i.e., "on the mouth") and not in writing (Gittin 60b). The rabbinic excuse was that "al-pi" (על-פי), which means "in accordance," resembles the word "Al-Pe" (על-פה), which means "upon the mouth." Therefore, the correct interpretation of this text, according to the Talmud, is as an allusion to the Oral Law.

2. The Bible makes it clear that the book of the Torah was fully completed in its written form (e.g., Deut 31:24–26; Josh 8:34–35; 2 Kings 22:8–11; Neh 8:1–3). But a Midrash, called "Degel Mahaneh Ephraim" (דגל מחנה אפרים), argued that the Written Law is not completed without the Oral Law; rather, it is only half a book. Thus, the Torah is only complete with both the Written Law and the Oral Law combined.[210] "Midrash Shmuel"[211] explains that God did not give Moses the entire Torah, for he was not ready enough to receive it. Therefore, the Written Law is only a fraction of the whole Torah, which includes the vast Oral Law.[212]

3. Psalm 119:126 says: "It is time for thee, LORD, to work; for they have made void thy law" (עֵת לַעֲשׂוֹת לַה' הֵפֵרוּ תּוֹרָתֶךָ). The whole chapter is praising the Lord's commandments and therefore, from the context, it is understood that the plain intention of the verse is to say that instead of doing God's will, they have broken His

[210]See in: Bazak, A. (in Hebrew):
אמנון בזק, עד היום הזה, בהוצאת: משכל (ידיעות ספרים), 2013, עמ' 416

[211] מדרש שמואל על מסכת אבות א'
[212]See discussion in: Rawidowicz, Simon (in Hebrew):
שמעון ראבידוביץ, עיונים במחשבת ישראל – כרך ראשון, הוצאת ראובן מס בע"מ, ירושלים, 1969, עמ' 46-47

law.[213] The Babylonian Talmud completely twisted this meaning by arguing it refers to the Oral Law, saying that although it was forbidden to write the Oral Law, the Sages had to write it so it would not be forgotten. In other words, sometimes you must break the Law, in order to keep it (T'murah 14b). Additionally, another question begged to be asked; if the Oral Law can be forgotten, how can we trust that what we have today is not missing or broken?

4. Deuteronomy 16:20 says: "That which is altogether just shalt thou follow, that thou mayest live, and inherit the land which the LORD thy God giveth thee" (צֶדֶק צֶדֶק תִּרְדֹּף לְמַעַן תִּחְיֶה וְיָרַשְׁתָּ אֶת־הָאָרֶץ אֲשֶׁר־ה' אֱלֹהֶיךָ נֹתֵן לָךְ). The context refers to justice in the legal sense and to the basic demand of the judges and officers, who are appointed in verse 18, to do their best to maintain true and uncompromising justice.[214] The Sages ignored the plain sense of the verse and used it in order to command attendance at the yeshiva (b. Talmud, Sanhedrin 32b). Thus, the Torah says, "Pursue righteousness"! The rabbis say, "Pursue us, the righteous ones, to the yeshiva"![215]

[213]"Psalms," part 2, in "World of the Bible" encyclopedia – (in Hebrew):
נחום מ. סרנה (עורך), עולם התנ"ך - תהלים ב', דברי הימים הוצאה לאור בע"מ, רעננה, 1993-1996, עמ' 209

[214]"Deuteronomy," in "World of the Bible" encyclopedia – (in Hebrew):
משה וינפלד וכהן-צמח דוד (עורכים), עולם התנ"ך – דברים, דברי הימים הוצאה לאור בע"מ, רעננה, , עמ' 2002, עמ' 139

[215]See: Rosenfeld, B., in: Gafni, I., Oppenheimer, A. Stern, M. (eds.), in Hebrew:
בן-ציון רוזנפלד, בתוך: מנחם שטרן, ישעיהו גפני ואהרן אופנהיימר, (עורכים), יהודים ויהדות בימי בית שני, המשנה והתלמוד, בהוצאת: יד יצחק בן-צבי, ירושלים, 1993, עמ' 159

5. Deuteronomy 32:25 says, "Outside the sword will bereave, and inside terror—
both young man and virgin, the nursling with the man of gray hair" (מִחוּץ תְּשַׁכֶּל־חֶרֶב וּמֵחֲדָרִים אֵימָה גַּם־בָּחוּר גַּם־בְּתוּלָה יוֹנֵק עִם־אִישׁ שֵׂיבָה). According to the plain contextual meaning, the object of grief and terror will be men, women, children, and elderly people. "Midrash Tanaim" (מדרש תנאים) to Deuteronomy 32 deliberately added the Hebrew letter *yud* (יוד) to the word, "elderly" (שֵׂיבָה), and by doing so, changed it to mean yeshiva (ישיבה), as if to say, "everyone should go to yeshiva." In this case, the rabbis changed both the text and the meaning of the Torah, to suit their agenda.

6. Genesis 49:13–14 says: "Zebulun will dwell at the seashore; and he *shall be* a haven for ships, and his flank *shall be* toward Sidon. Issachar is a strong donkey, lying down between the sheepfolds" (זְבוּלֻן לְחוֹף יַמִּים יִשְׁכֹּן וְהוּא לְחוֹף אֳנִיֹּת וְיַרְכָתוֹ עַל־צִידֹן. יִשָּׂשכָר חֲמֹר גָּרֶם רֹבֵץ בֵּין הַמִּשְׁפְּתָיִם). The word, "sheepfolds," could mean either "sheep pens" or "cooking stoves."[216] But this did not prevent the Sages to interpret the verse as if it indicates that Issachar was learning Talmud in the yeshiva, while his brother financed his studies (Midrash Bereshit Raba, V'Yehi 98–99).[217] The rabbis took it even further and treated this alleged agreement between the brothers as a precedent which gave future yeshiva students justification to learn the Talmud at

[216]See Kadari, 680.

[217] מדרש בראשית רבה, פרשת ויחי צ"ח-צ"ט

the expense of someone else's hard labor.[218]

7. Job 11:7–9 says: "Can you discover the depths of God? Can you discover the limits of the Almighty? *They are* high as the heavens, what can you do? Deeper than Sheol, what can you know? Its measure is longer than the earth and broader than the sea" (הַחֵקֶר אֱלוֹהַ תִּמְצָא אִם עַד־תַּכְלִית שַׁדַּי תִּמְצָא. גָּבְהֵי שָׁמַיִם מַה־תִּפְעָל עֲמֻקָּה מִשְּׁאוֹל מַה־תֵּדָע. אֲרֻכָּה מֵאֶרֶץ מִדָּהּ וּרְחָבָה מִנִּי־יָם). This simply means that God's wisdom is greater than the earth and wider than the sea.[219] But in an ongoing effort to justify learning Talmud in the yeshiva, the Sages interpreted verse nine as referring to the Oral Law (Midrash Tanhuma 58:3).[220] By doing so, they misinterpreted the Bible in at least three ways: 1) They completely ignored the contextual meaning of the verse. 2) They have inserted the Oral Law in to the book of Job, even though it never hints at such an idea.[221] 3) In this midrash, the rabbis quote a verse which was spoken by Job's friend, Zophar the Naamathite (v. 1). But in Job 42:7 God Himself says to Eliphaz the Temanite that he and his two friends (including Zophar) did not say the right things to Job. Therefore, even if the rabbis' interpretation was valid, it is still based upon a false position.

---

[218]See in: Rosenthal, 55; and also: Zicherman, H. (in Hebrew):
חיים זיכרמן, שחור כחול לבן: מסע אל תוך החברה החרדית בישראל, משכל (ידיעות ספרים), 2014, עמ' 191

[219]Nebentzal, Y. (in Hebrew):
ישעיהו נבנצל, איש תם וישר: לימוד ועיון בספר איוב, הוצאת ראובן מס בע"מ, ירושלים, 2008, עמ' 143

[220] מדרש תנחומא נ"ח ג'

[221]The book of Job probably predates Moses' time, and therefore does not even mention the Written Law, let alone the Oral Law. See "Job," in "World of the Bible" encyclopedia (in Hebrew):
עולם התנ"ך – איוב, דברי הימים הוצאה לאור בע"מ, רעננה, 1993-1996, עמ' 16

8. Deuteronomy 6:7 says: "You shall teach them diligently to your sons and shall talk of them when you sit in your house and when you walk by the way and when you lie down and when you rise up" (וְשִׁנַּנְתָּם לְבָנֶיךָ וְדִבַּרְתָּ בָּם בְּשִׁבְתְּךָ בְּבֵיתֶךָ וּבְלֶכְתְּךָ בַדֶּרֶךְ וּבְשָׁכְבְּךָ וּבְקוּמֶךָ). In an attempt to justify the Oral Law, the rabbis changed the phrase "teach them diligently" (וְשִׁנַּנְתָּם), to say: "three times" (ושלשתם). Why three? Because a man must divide his days into three parts: one third should be devoted for the Torah; the second third for the Mishnah; the final third for the Talmud (b. Talmud, Kiddushin 30a). This is yet another classic example of the liberty the rabbis took in order to use the Bible for their own purposes; not only that they changed a word in the holy text, they also added a commandment which does not appear in the Torah (according to which, a man must learn the Mishnah and the Talmud, two thirds of the time).

9. Numbers 31:3–5 says: "Moses spoke to the people, saying, 'Arm men from among you for the war, that they may go against Midian to execute the Lord's vengeance on Midian. A thousand from each tribe of all the tribes of Israel you shall send to the war.' So there were furnished from the thousands of Israel, a thousand from each tribe, twelve thousand armed for war." (וַיְדַבֵּר מֹשֶׁה אֶל־הָעָם לֵאמֹר הֵחָלְצוּ מֵאִתְּכֶם אֲנָשִׁים לַצָּבָא וְיִהְיוּ עַל־מִדְיָן לָתֵת נִקְמַת־ה' בְּמִדְיָן. אֶלֶף לַמַּטֶּה אֶלֶף לַמַּטֶּה לְכֹל מַטּוֹת יִשְׂרָאֵל תִּשְׁלְחוּ לַצָּבָא. וַיִּמָּסְרוּ מֵאַלְפֵי יִשְׂרָאֵל אֶלֶף לַמַּטֶּה שְׁנֵים־עָשָׂר אֶלֶף חֲלוּצֵי צָבָא). Midrash B'Midbar Rabba 22 boldly contradicted this text by saying Moses sent two thousand or even three thousand men of each tribe and not merely one thousand. Why? Because the Sages sought to use this passage in order to prove that winning the war is dependent on those who study Talmud in yeshivas.[222]

10. Psalm 15:4 says: "In whose eyes a reprobate is despised, but who honors those who fear the Lord; he swears to his own hurt and does not change" (נִבְזֶה בְּעֵינָיו נִמְאָס וְאֶת־יִרְאֵי ה' יְכַבֵּד נִשְׁבַּע לְהָרַע וְלֹא יָמִר). With total disregard for the context, the Babylonian Talmud[223] decided this verse must be speaking about King Jehoshaphat, who—according to the Sages—used to stand on his feet every time he saw a "wise disciple" (תלמיד-חכם) and then kissed and hugged him, saying, "rabbi, rabbi, master, master."

11. Genesis 18:8 says: "He took curds and milk and the calf which he had prepared, and placed *it* before them; and he was standing by them under the tree as they ate" (וַיִּקַּח חֶמְאָה וְחָלָב וּבֶן־הַבָּקָר אֲשֶׁר עָשָׂה וַיִּתֵּן לִפְנֵיהֶם וְהוּא־עֹמֵד עֲלֵיהֶם תַּחַת הָעֵץ וַיֹּאכֵלוּ). Clearly, according to the text, Abraham was standing before his guests when they ate. But in order to prove from the Bible that everyone should stand on their feet when they see a rabbi, the Sages took this passage and have turned the meaning upside down.[224] Instead of Abraham standing by God, the rabbis argued that the Shekinah (השכינה) stood before Abraham; by doing so, God has fulfilled

[222]Zicherman, 320.

[223]Tractate Ketubot 103b (in Hebrew):
יהושפט מלך יהודה, כשהיה רואה תלמיד חכם היה עומד מכסאו ומחבקו ומנשקו וקורא לו: רבי רבי, מרי מרי

[224]In Midrash Bereshit Rabba 48 (מדרש בראשית רבה מ"ח).

the rabbinic commandment of "standing before the elder [rabbi]," and gave an example for the way by which future generations should give honor to the rabbis.[225]

12. Numbers 27:18–21 says:

So the Lord said to Moses, "Take Joshua the son of Nun . . . and lay your hand on him; and have him stand before Eleazar the priest and before all the congregation . . . . You shall put some of your authority on him, in order that all the congregation of the sons of Israel may obey *him*. . . . At his command they shall go out and at his command they shall come in, *both* he and the sons of Israel with him, even all the congregation." (קַח־לְךָ אֶת־יְהוֹשֻׁעַ בִּן־נוּן... וְהַעֲמַדְתָּ אֹתוֹ לִפְנֵי אֶלְעָזָר הַכֹּהֵן וְלִפְנֵי כָּל־הָעֵדָה וְצִוִּיתָה אֹתוֹ לְעֵינֵיהֶם וְנָתַתָּה מֵהוֹדְךָ עָלָיו לְמַעַן יִשְׁמְעוּ כָּל־עֲדַת בְּנֵי יִשְׂרָאֵל... וְלִפְנֵי אֶלְעָזָר הַכֹּהֵן יַעֲמֹד... הוּא וְכָל־בְּנֵי־יִשְׂרָאֵל אִתּוֹ וְכָל־הָעֵדָה).

The phrase "all the congregation" (כל העדה) is obviously referring to all the children of Israel (see vv. 2 and 20 in the same chapter). But the Sages wanted to justify the function of the Sanhedrin (which they ruled),[226] and therefore said, "'all the congregation,' this is the Sanhedrin" (b. Talmud, Yoma 73b). This interpretation seems even more extreme considering the fact that all through the Bible, the phrase, "all the congregation," refers only to Israel, and never to a distinct body, such as the Sanhedrin. But that did not

[225]In Hebrew, this law is called Amidat-Zaken (עמידת זקן). See: Averbach, 169.

[226]Levin, I. L., in: Barkai, G. & Shiller, E. (eds.), 136–38.

prevent the Sages from repeating the same intentional error when they interpreted Exodus 19:3 to say: "'Thus you shall say to the house of Jacob,' these are the Sanhedrin."[227] Of course, the term "the house of Jacob" (בֵּית יַעֲקֹב) has nothing to do with the Sanhedrin, but simply means "the children of Israel" (Exod. 19:3).

These examples do not merely reflect a distorted interpretation of the Bible, but rather clear and intentional misinterpretations which prove that the rabbis did not mind twisting the Torah as long as it suited their agenda; i.e., to establish the case for the Oral Law and their alleged God-given authority over Israel, justifying it through the authoritative legacy of the Bible.[228]

The sages use several proof-texts from the Bible in order to prove the validity of the Oral Law and their alleged authority over Israel. We will now refute four of the most significant claims which they use:

1. Exodus 34:27 reads: "Then the Lord said to Moses, 'Write down these words, for in accordance with these words I have made a covenant with you and with Israel.'" The words, "for in accordance with these words," in Hebrew is: כְּתָב־לְךָ אֶת־הַדְּבָרִים הָאֵלֶּה כִּי עַל־פִּי הַדְּבָרִים הָאֵלֶּה. But although this verse clearly says that the covenant is based upon the written

[227]Midrash Shmot Raba, 'Seder Jethro' 28, in Hebrew: מדרש שמות רבה, 'סדר יתרו', פרשה כ"ח

[228]See: Gafni, C. (in Hebrew):
חנן גפני, 'פשוטה של משנה': עיונים בחקר ספרות חז"ל בעת החדשה, בהוצאת: הקיבוץ המאוחד, רעננה, 2011, עמ' 192

words,[229] the rabbis took the Hebrew phrase עַל־פִּי ("in accordance") and turned it into עַל-פֶּה (meaning: "orally").[230] Ironically, the Sages used one of the clearest verses of the Torah that points to the Written Law, in order to prove the Oral Law.

2. Deuteronomy 17:8–11 says:

If any case is too difficult for you to decide, between one kind of homicide or another, between one kind of lawsuit or another, and between one kind of assault or another, being cases of dispute in your courts, then you shall arise and go up to the place which the Lord your God chooses. So you shall come to the Levitical priest or the judge who is *in office* in those days, and you shall inquire *of them* and they will declare to you the verdict in the case. You shall do according to the terms of the verdict which they declare to you from that place which the Lord chooses; and you shall be careful to observe according to all that they teach you. According to the terms of the law which they teach you, and according to the verdict which they tell you, you shall do; you shall not turn aside from the word which they declare to you, to the right or the left.

The rabbis used this portion as a proof of their God-given authority over Israel through the Sanhedrin, for the present and for the future.[231] They took verse 11 even further, to claim that even when they tell you that right is left and left is

---

[229]Kadari, 799, 848.

[230]b. Talmud, Gittin 60b.

[231]b. Talmud, Sotta 45a. See discussion in: Ofer, 267; and also in: Gilat, Y. D. (in Hebrew): יצחק ד' גילת, פרקים בהשתלשלות ההלכה, הוצאת אוניברסיטת בר אילן, 1992, עמ' 344

right—and you know it's wrong—still, you must obey them.[232]

But here are a few fatal problems with that exegesis:

A. We have already shown that in contrast to what the Sages claim, the Sanhedrin was established only in the Second Temple Period, and not before.

B. The passage begins by saying that only when an individual is faced with a specific legal dispute, only then should he go, at his own initiative, to the judge to find resolution (v. 8). Nowhere do these verses give the judges any liberty to legislate new laws; instead, they simply instruct them to rule according to the Written Law (v. 11).[233] According to this passage, the role of the judges is merely to judge by the law of the Torah and not to add countless new laws which in most cases have nothing to do with the Written Law.

C. The Sages believe that "the judge" (v. 9) refers to the rabbis themselves, but they fail to acknowledge that in the biblical era the priests also served as judges. Legal matters were often associated with the Temple, and so it was natural for the priests to engage in implementing judgment.[234] Thus, there is no reason

---

[232]Midrash Song of Song Rabba 1 (שיר השירים רבה א'). In his commentary on this verse, Nachmanides (רמב"ן) says that this is true even when you know they are wrong in there rulings; nevertheless, you must obey. In Hebrew:
אפילו אם אומר לך על ימין שהוא שמאל או על שמאל שהוא ימין, לשון רש"י, ועניינו אפילו תחשוב בלבך שהם טועים והדבר פשוט בעיניך כאשר אתה יודע בין ימינך לשמאלך – תעשה כמצוותם

[233]See also in contexts: v. 18–20.

[234]"Deuteronomy," in "World of the Bible" encyclopedia – (in Hebrew):

to assume that it refers to the rabbis/ Pharisees, which are first mentioned towards the end of the Second Temple era.[235]

D. The Babylonian Talmud (Nida 19a) interpreted "between blood and blood" (v. 8) as if to say, "between matters of impurity and purity; pure blood and impure blood." But the genuine contextual meaning of the verse is not between kinds of blood; rather, it refers to criminal law, to cases of killings, murder, etc.[236] This clearly demonstrates how this specific text could not have given the rabbis any authority to rule, for they could not even figure out its authentic contextual meaning.

E. Throughout the Bible, the priests were the ones who were given the Torah; they were responsible for teaching the Written Law to Israel; and they were responsible to preserve it in order to pass it on to future generations;[237] therefore, they knew best how to implement the Torah and to judge according to it.

3. According to another common argument made by the rabbis, there is no way to know how to keep the Written Law without the interpretation of the Oral

---

משה וינפלד וכהן-צמח דוד (עורכים), עולם התנ"ך – דברים, דברי הימים הוצאה לאור בע"מ, רעננה, 2002, עמ' 142

[235]Rapoport, Uriel. in: Stern, Menachem (ed.), in Hebrew:
רפפורט, א., בתוך: מנחם שטרן, (עורך), ההיסטוריה של ארץ-ישראל – התקופה ההלניסטית ומדינת החשמונאים (332 - 37 לפני הספירה), יד יצחק בן-צבי, כתר הוצאה לאור, ירושלים, 1981, עמ' 256-257

[236]See: Tigay, J. H. (in Hebrew):
יעקב טיגאי, מקרא לישראל: פירוש מדעי למקרא - דברים - כרך שני טז, יח – לד, יב, בהוצאת: האוניברסיטה העברית בירושלים, עם עובד י"ל מאגנס, 2016, עמ' 456
And: Werman, C. & Shemesh, A., 73; and also: "Deuteronomy," in "World of the Bible" encyclopaedia, 142 – in Hebrew.

[237]Elior, 150–52.

Law. Keeping the Sabbath is one example which they often give. How can one rest from all work unless he knows the right definition of "work"?[238]

There are several simple answers to this question:

A. As pointed out several times already, the Levitical priests were the ones to whom the mandate to uphold the Torah was given. In fact, in a discussion about the Sabbath law, the Babylonian Talmud itself admits that the priests were quick and cautious in regard to keeping the commandments.[239] Hence, if there were any questions in regard to keeping the Sabbath laws, the people of Israel knew they could trust the priests and count on them to give the right instructions.

B. The Torah itself proves that there was no Oral Law upon which Moses could consult in regard to implementing the Written Law. Numbers 15:32–36 gives an account of a man who had been caught gathering wood on the Sabbath and was put "in custody because it had not been declared what should be done to him" (v. 34). Thereafter, God instructed Moses to stone this man to death (v. 35). This account raises serious questions concerning the Oral Law:

---

[238]Lau, Israel M., in his book: "Foundations – One Hundred Concepts in Judaism" (in Hebrew): ישראל מאיר לאו, הנחת יסוד: מאה מושגים ביהדות, בהוצאת: משכל (ידיעות ספרים), 2008, עמ' 33

[239]Tractate Shabbat 20a (see Rabbi Adin Steinsaltz commentary).

1) If Moses had already received the interpretation of the Oral Law, why didn't he know that this man deserved to be stoned?

2) The Babylonian Talmud (Sanhedrin 78b) says Moses did not know the kind of death by which the man deserved to be killed. But this does not make any sense because according to the Oral Law, the kind of death in this incident must be by stoning.[240] Therefore, if this issue is clearly mentioned in the Oral Law, it must have been given to Moses, together with the Written Law, as the rabbis repeatedly claim.[241] Moses however, did not know how to act, but had to consult with God in order to receive the right action. Conclusion: obviously, there was no Oral Law given to him in which he could find answers.

3) The Torah gives at least four other accounts where Moses had waited to hear from God, because he did not know how to apply the Torah under the given circumstances (Lev 24:12; Num 9:8; 16:5; 27:5). If the interpretation of the Written Law was given to him in the form of the Oral Law and passed on to the seventy elders, Moses would not have had to rely upon hearing from God. Rather, he should have handled the situation just like the

---

[240]Maimonides, Mishneh Torah, Shabbat 1.

[241]As stated in j. Talmud 28a.

Talmud did, in tractate Baba Metzia 59b, for instance.

4) The rabbinic literature argues that Israel has never successfully fulfilled the Written Law but rather, always managed to keep the Oral Law alone.[242] This does not make any biblical sense whatsoever, for one simple reason: as shown above, the rabbis claim that the Written Law cannot be fulfilled without the interpretation of the Oral Law, which was given with it on Sinai.[243] But if Israel had the guidance of the Oral Law already, how could they break the Written Law? If the Oral Law explains the Torah and you break the written commandments, it means you also broke the Oral Law. In other words, it is not possible to keep the Oral Law on one hand and to break the Written Law on the other hand. If the Written Law and the Oral Law are one and the same, when you break one you break the other as well.

C. Also, the rabbis argue that without the Oral Law there is no way to keep other commandments of the Torah, such as circumcision (מילה), menstruation (נידה), or kosher slaughtering (שחיטה כשרה); but biblical scholars have proven that the priests knew exactly how to perform

---

[242]Minhat Eliyahu, chapter 2 (in Hebrew: ספר "מנחת אליהו", פרק ב, עמ' 30-31)

[243]Lau, Israel M, 32–35.

and uphold these laws with no help from an alleged Oral Law.[244]

4. A different argument claims that the only way we can read and understand the Tanakh is in accordance with the Hebrew punctuation method (ניקוד), which was passed on orally to the Sages.[245] But after a linguistic-historical examination, this argument turns out to be no less ludicrous than the former claims.

Most scholars believe that the biblical punctuation system, as known today, developed no earlier than the ninth century AD, most probably in Tiberias (טבריה). Some argue that it was even invented there.[246] It is quite clear that the punctuation came into existence only after the Talmudic period, for it never appears there.[247] In fact, the research recognizes two major competing systems of punctuation: the "Babylonian" method and the "Tiberian" method. Around the end of the 10th century the latter method took over and became the dominant one.[248]

---

[244]Mazar, Benjamin (ed.), "Biblical Encyclopedia" (in Hebrew):
בנימין מזר (עורך), אנציקלופדיה מקראית: אוצר הידיעות של המקרא ותקופתו - ה: ממובן – סתרי, בהוצאת: מוסד ביאליק, ירושלים, 1968, עמ' 785
בנימין מזר (עורך), שם, ד: כבד – מלתחה, 1962, עמ' 896-898
See also: Rubin, Nissan. (in Hebrew):
ניסן רובין, ראשית החיים, בהוצאת: הקיבוץ המאוחד, רעננה, 2005, עמ' 77-78
And also: Keren, Rachel, In: Keren, R. (ed.), in Hebrew:
רחל קרן (עורכת), השמיעיני את קולך: עיונים במעגל השנה ובפרשות השבוע, הוצאת ראובן מס בע"מ, ירושלים, 2009, עמ' 236

[245]See: Gillis, Miriam (in Hebrew):
מרים גיליס, היבטים חדשים בהוראה מתקנת, הוצאת דקל - פרסומים אקדמיים בע"מ, 1978, עמ' 19
And also: Benjamin Mazar, ed., *Biblical Encyclopaedia* (in Hebrew):
בנימין מזר (עורך), שם, ה: ממובן – סתרי, 1968, עמ' 839

[246]Kimchi, Israel, in: Biger, Gideon & Shiller, Eli (eds.), in Hebrew:
ישראל קמחי, בתוך: גדעון ביגר ואלי שילר (עורכים), אריאל: כתב עת לידיעת ארץ ישראל – טבריה וסביבתה, הוצאת ספרים אריאל, ירושלים, 1987, עמ' 9

[247]Mazar, Benjamin (ed.), 840–41.

The punctuation signs under the Hebrew text were written in the following manner: First, a scribe would carefully copy the text, and only then a different scholar would go over it and insert the punctuation.[249] Therefore, the biblical punctuation system is considered not merely to be a guide that helps in reading the text, but also as a tendentious interpretive tool that expresses the understanding of the punctuator, rather than an ancient oral tradition allegedly passed down from Moses.[250]

Moreover, as emphasized before, throughout the Bible we read that the Levitical priests were given the mandate to read the Torah to Israel; they alone were in charge of teaching and imparting it to the people. And they were given the responsibility to preserve the text, to copy it, and to transmit it to future generations.[251] Thus, even if there were an oral tradition according to which the Torah was being read, it would have belonged to the Priests and had nothing to do with the rabbinic Oral Law.

---

[248] Ibid., 842–45.

[249] Rosenthal, Yemima & Tsoref, Hagai (eds.), in Hebrew:
חגי צורף וימימה רוזנטל (עורכים), יצחק בן-צבי: הנשיא השני, בהוצאת: ארכיון המדינה, 1998, עמ' 506

[250] Tur-Sinai, Naftali, Hertz. *The Language and the Book* (in Hebrew):
נפתלי הרץ טור-סיני, הלשון והספר: בעיות יסוד במדע הלשון ובמקורותיה הספרותיים - כרך הספר, בהוצאת: מוסד ביאליק, ירושלים, 1959, עמ' 16

[251] Elior, 150.

Chapter 8

THE ORAL LAW AND THE NEW TESTAMENT

The previous chapter showed how disconnected the Oral Law is from the Tanakh. But what about the New Testament (NT) writings? Some rabbis, and even a few well known Messianic scholars, argue that Yeshua was a devout Pharisee, who not only recognized rabbinic authority, but also observed the Oral Law. Therefore, they claim, even Messianic Jews today are obligated to keep the Oral Law.[252]

Hence, this chapter will evaluate the validity of this claim. After all, didn't Yeshua Himself tell us to listen to the rabbis and follow their laws? Matthew 23:2–3, says: "The scribes and the Pharisees sit on Moses' seat, so do and observe whatever they tell you"? Let us now address this issue in an organized fashion, by laying down several key points.[253]

[252]See: Dauermann, Stuart. *The Rabbi as a Surrogate Priest*. Eugene, Wipf & Stock Pub., 2009; Harvey, Richard. *Mapping Messianic Jewish Theology: A Constructive Approach*. Colorado Springs, Paternoster, 2009; Kinzer, Mark S. *Postmissionary Messianic Judaism: Redefining Christian Engagement with the Jewish People*. Grand Rapids, Brazos Press, 2005; and also: Stern, David H. Messianic Jewish Manifesto. Jerusalem, Messianic Jewish Resources International, 1988.

[253]Mostly taken from: Seth Postell, Eitan Bar, and Erez Soref, *Reading Moses, Seeing Jesus: How the Torah Fulfils its Goal in Jesus* (Netanya, Israel: ONE FOR ISRAEL Ministry, 2015).

1. It is not wise to build a comprehensive theology upon a single verse, especially one taken out of context. At this point in Matthew's Gospel, Yeshua is speaking before the inauguration of the New Covenant. After all, if Yeshua wanted us to follow the rabbis (Pharisees and scribes), he would have mentioned it somewhere else in the Gospels.

2. Yeshua demonstrates in His own life the exact opposite of this. He does not wash His hands according to the traditions of Second Temple Judaism (Matt 15:1–9). Elsewhere He clearly states: "You are experts at setting aside the commandment of God in order to keep your tradition" (Mark 7:9). The idea that God despises man-made religious traditions as a means to gain His favor is not new. We see it throughout the Bible (e.g., Isa. 29:13).

3. If Yeshua is suggesting in a single verse that we must obey the rabbis, He forgot to inform us which rabbinical sect to follow (e.g., the house of Shammai or the house of Hillel), for they often represented opposing interpretations of the Law in Yeshua's day. Furthermore, Yeshua would be in direct contradiction with the prophets and even with His own teaching in the same chapter, as we will see.

4. What did Yeshua mean by saying "Moses' seat"? Does it refer to rabbinic authority as some have argued? No! Rather, "Moses' seat" refers to the physical place in the synagogue where the Scriptures were read.[254]

---

[254]See: Ilan, Zvi, in: Shiller, Eli (ed.), in Hebrew:
צבי אילן, בתוך: אלי שילר (עורך), אריאל: כתב עת לידיעת ארץ ישראל - בתי-כנסת בגליל ובגולן, הוצאת ספרים אריאל, ירושלים, 1987, עמ' 115

Support for this interpretation can be found in a village north of the Sea of Galilee called Chorazin.[255] In an ancient synagogue, dating from the fourth century, archaeologists discovered something called "Moses' seat," a seat in the synagogue where the Hebrew Scriptures were read aloud. Though the inscriptions at this site are from a later period, it is safe to assume this custom did not suddenly appear out of the blue in the fourth century.[256]

When Yeshua tells the people of Israel to listen to the scribes and Pharisees when they read from Moses' seat, He means it in a literal way. And why is it so important to Yeshua that the people of Israel listen to the Scriptures being read? Yeshua knows that the Scriptures point to Him: "For if you believed Moses, you would believe Me, for he wrote about Me" (John 5:46). Moses' seat in the synagogue was the only place from which a Jewish person in the Second Temple Period could hear Moses and the Prophets bear testimony concerning the Messiah. For example, Torah says, "The Lord your God will raise up for you a prophet like me from among you, from your countrymen, you shall listen to him" (Deut. 18:15). Yeshua wants the people of Israel to listen to Moses, because Moses points to Him.[257]

---

[255]Tepper, Yigal and Tepper, Yotam. The Road that Bears the People (in Hebrew):
יגאל טפר ויותם טפר, דרכים נושאות עם, בהוצאת: הקיבוץ המאוחד, רעננה, 2013, עמ' 190

[256]Hananel Mack of Bar-Ilan University's Talmudic Department affirms that the New Testament's "Seat of Moses" is referring to the physical seat from which Scriptures were read inside the synagogue. He bases this both on modern archaeological findings and on the ancient rabbinic commentary Pesikta de-Rab Kahana 7b. See Mack, Hananel, (in Hebrew):
חננאל מאק, "קתדרה דמשה וקתדרה דדרושה", קתדרה: כתב עת לתולדות ארץ ישראל ויישובה, חוברת 72 (יוני 1994): 3-12

[257]Maimonides (Mishneh Torah, Hilchot Melachim and Wars 11:2) affirms that the whole Torah has been testifying directly to the Messiah (in Hebrew): וכל מי שאינו מאמין בו, או מי שאינו מחכה לביאתו – לא בשאר נביאים בלבד הוא כופר, אלא בתורה ובמשה רבנו: שהרי תורה העידה עליו

5. In the same chapter (Matt 23), He accuses the Pharisees and scribes of being “hypocrites” (v. 13), “child[ren] of hell” (v. 15), “blind guides” (v. 16), “blind fools” (v. 17), “full of hypocrisy and lawlessness” (v. 28), “serpents” and “a brood of vipers” (v. 33), and murderers (v. 35). Do we seriously think Yeshua commands us to follow them? Yeshua clearly states that they are respecting man-made traditions over God’s Word! (Matt 15:9, quoting Isa 29:13). When Yeshua says, “The scribes and the Pharisees sit on Moses’ seat, so do and observe whatever they tell you, but not the works they do” (Matt 23:2–3, emphasis added), He is referring to those man-made traditions they promote in the name of God (later called the Oral Law). Matthew 23 in its entirety shows us that Yeshua opposes man-made religion and traditions as a way to reach God.

6. If Yeshua were telling us to obey the scribes and Pharisees we would have an even bigger dilemma. For the Oral Law directly contradicts the teachings of Yeshua. The Babylonian Talmud teaches not only that Yeshua is a false prophet but also that when supposedly contacted through sorcery after His death, Yeshua is asked about His fate; He allegedly replies that He is suffering in hell, “in boiling excrement” (Gittin 57a).[258]

---

[258]In fact, throughout the present copies of the Talmud, Yeshua’s name is deliberately written as an acronym which expresses a curse. Interestingly enough, a rare copy of the B. Talmud, tractate Sanhedrin 43a – preserved by the exiled Yemenite Jews – reveals a different version than the norm. Here, the name is actually Yeshua (ישוע), instead of the typical Yeshu (יש"ו), which appears in most common versions. See discussion in: Yosef Tobi, Jacob Barnai, and Shalom Bar-Asher, “History of the Jews in the Islamic Countries” (in Hebrew):

7. Several times in the Gospels it says that Yeshua opened the Scriptures and showed His followers all that was written about Him (Matt 5:17, 21:42; Luke 16:31, 24:44–45; John 5:39, 46).[259] But never did Yeshua say to them, "search the writings of Moses and of the Prophets, and also the traditional oral teaching of the Scribes and Pharisees, and you shall find me there—they have all spoke of me." In other words, Yeshua said that Moses spoke of Him, but He never suggested that His disciples should search the Oral Law traditions, and that they would find Him there.

8. Yeshua specifically told His disciples to beware of the teachings and traditions of the Pharisees (Matt 16:11–12; Mark 7:1–13; Luke 12:1). And even if Yeshua had acknowledged an alleged Oral Law given from Sinai, even then, the rabbis themselves claim that the Torah of Moses will be replaced[260] by a new Torah given through the Messiah![261] In fact, even some

---

יוסף טובי, יעקב ברנאי ושלום בר-אשר, תולדות היהודים בארצות האיסלאם, בהוצאת: מרכז זלמן שזר לחקר תולדות העם היהודי, ירושלים, 1981, עמ' 3-5
And also in: Yosef Tobi, in: Yaffa Berlowitz, ed., in Hebrew:
יוסף טובי, בתוך: יפה ברלוביץ (עורכת), לשוחח תרבות עם העלייה הראשונה: עיון בין התקופות, בהוצאת: הקיבוץ המאוחד, רעננה, 2010, עמ' 30-35

[259]See further discussion in: Michael Rydelnik, *The Messianic Hope: Is the Hebrew Bible Really Messianic?* (Nashville, TN: B&H Academic, 2010), 1–12.

[260]See Midrash Tehilim 146 (מדרש תהלים, מזמור קמ"ו); and see discussion in: David Brezis, in Hebrew:
דוד ברזיס, בין קנאות לחסד: מגמות אנטי־קנאיות במחשבת חז"ל, הוצאת אוניברסיטת בר אילן, 2015, עמ' 150-151
And in: Joseph Dan, in Hebrew:
יוסף דן, ר' יהודה החסיד, בהוצאת: מרכז זלמן שזר לחקר תולדות העם היהודי, ירושלים, 2006, עמ' 75
And also in: Levinger, Jacobs S. (in Hebrew):
יעקב לוינגר, הרמב"ם כפילוסוף וכפוסק, בהוצאת: מוסד ביאליק, ירושלים, 1989, עמ' 62

[261]Midrash Yalkut Shimoni, sign 429 (מדרש ילקוט שמעוני, ישעיהו כ"ו, רמז תכ"ט). See also: Benmelech, Moti, in: Ilan, N., Horowitz, K. & Kaplan, K. (eds.), in Hebrew:
מוטי בנמלך, בתוך: נחם אילן, קימי קפלן וכרמי הורוביץ (עורכים), דורש טוב לעמו: הדרשן, הדרשה וספרות הדרוש בתרבות היהודית, בהוצאת: מרכז זלמן שזר לחקר תולדות העם היהודי, ירושלים, 2012, עמ' 73-74

contemporary Orthodox rabbis affirm this.[262] So in any case, even the Sages have argued that once the Messiah comes, we are obligated to his government; to his interpretation of the law.[263]

9. None of the epistles ever encourage believers to obey an alleged Oral Law.

10. Following man-made laws or rabbinic traditions, as believers, not only misses the point of the Torah,[264] but also confuses both believers and non-believers. We cannot become "more Jewish" or draw nearer to God by following human traditions. It's either knowing God's righteousness through the Messiah, or establishing our own righteousness and submitting to it. Sadly, the rabbis chose the latter.[265]

---

[262]See: Dov Schwartz, "Habad's Thought: From Beginig to End" (in Hebrew):
דב שוורץ, מחשבת חב"ד: מראשית ועד אחרית, בהוצאת אוניברסיטת בר אילן, 2010, עמ' 395
And also see the link below to an article which quotes R. Joseph Telushkin, allegedly claiming that if the followers of Chabad (חב"ד) truly believed their Rebbe was the King Messiah, they would cease from keeping Moses' Torah. https://web.archive.org/web/20150319010954/http://roshpinaproject.com/2015/03/16/rabbi-telushkin-if-jews-believed-messiah-has-come-they-wouldnt-keep-torah/

[263]Midrash Elijah Zuta 20 (מדרש אליהו זוטא כ').

[264]Postell, Seth, Bar, Eitan & Soref, Erez, ibid, have shown that the purpose of the Torah has been fulfilled in Yeshua, as written in Rom. 10:4. Interestingly enough, even non-believing Jewish Bible Scholars have recently noticed that the Torah is more a narrative with laws which points to a specific purpose, than it is laws with little narrative. See: Avi Vershevski, Aviva Lotten, Roni Megidov & Ayala Paz (in Hebrew): אבי ורשבסקי, אביבה לוטן, רוני מגידוב ואילה פז, חוק וחברה במקרא: פרקי לימוד במקרא עם מדריך הכנה לבגרות, בהוצאת: מטח: המרכז לטכנולוגיה חינוכית, תל-אביב, 2005, עמ' 17-18

[265]See Rom 10:2–4.

Chapter 9

THE RABBINIC ATHEISTIC REVOLUTION

While maintaining a religious rhetoric and making use of some biblical phrases, the Sages managed to remove completely any dependency on a living God, on His Word, and on His Holy Spirit. Here are a few indications of the atheistic revolution they accomplished, by elevating their own status above that of God Himself, and by taking Him completely out of the religious sphere.

1. Revocation of the Holy Spirit: All through the Tanakh, the Holy Spirit (רוח הקודש) plays a vital role; we read this from Genesis 1:2, through Numbers 11:25, and in the book of Judges, where God raises up judges for Israel and fills them with His Spirit (e.g., Judges 3:10, 6:34, 11:29, 14:19). Nevertheless, the rabbis determined that when the last of the prophets died, the Holy Spirit left Israel.[266]

2. Abolition of Prophecy: In the Bible, the prophets served as a kind of barometer of Israel's spiritual status; as mediators between God and His people. So much so, that Amos (3:7) proclaimed that the Lord would do nothing, except through the revelation He would give to His

[266]Schwartz, Daniel, in: Naor, Mordechai (ed.), in Hebrew:
דניאל שוורץ, בתוך: מרדכי נאור (עורך), המלך הורדוס ותקופתו: מקורות, סיכומים, פרשיות נבחרות וחומר עזר, בהוצאת: יד יצחק בן-צבי, ירושלים, 1987, עמ' 42

servants the prophets. In fact, Moses wished all Israel would become prophets (Num 11:29), and Joel (3:1) had a future hope that God would pour out His Spirit upon all flesh and all Israel would prophesy. The Sages however, decided that from the day the Second Temple was destroyed, prophecy was taken from the prophets and was handed over to the rabbis.[267] But they went further, saying that without the Holy Spirit, there is no possibility of prophecy.[268] So first, the Sages ended the work of the Holy Spirit, and then they argued that there is no room for prophecy while the Spirit of God has ceased from working.

3. End of Obedience to the Voice from Heaven (בת קול): In a legal dispute between the Talmudic Sages, Rabbi Joshua declared that from now on there is no longer dependency on the voice from heaven, but rather in the majority rule of the Sages (b. Talmud, Baba Metzia 59b). This bold claim seems most revolutionary, especially since the some rabbis admit elsewhere that the voice from heaven does in fact reflect the will of God.[269]

4. Exemption from Dependency on the Supernatural: Some rabbinic traditions have rooted out all reliance upon the Holy Spirit, upon prophecy, and upon the voice from heaven. Interestingly enough, these three pillars have lost their validity, just as the rabbis were taking over the reins

---

[267] See in: Ahituv, Yosef, A Critique of Contemporary Religious Zionism – Selected Writings (in Hebrew): יוסף אחיטוב, משבי רוח: דברי הגות ומחשבה, בהוצאת: מכון שלום הרטמן, 2013, עמ' 219

[268] Menachem Haran, in Hebrew:
מנחם הרן, האסופה המקראית: תהליכי הגיבוש עד סוף ימי בית שני ושינויי הצורה עד מוצאי ימי הביניים - חלק א, מוסד ביאליק, האוניברסיטה העברית בירושלים, י"ל מאגנס, 1996, עמ' 74

[269] According to b. Talmud, Brachot 17b (see also in: Haran, 350-358; and: Gruber, 250–52).

of Israel. Was this a coincidence, or a deliberate action? In any case, this process led to the final shift of authority from the priests and the prophets, directly to the hands of the rabbis, while releasing all religious and legal decisions from any reliance on the supernatural.[270]

5. Reciting from the Siddur, Rather than Praying from the Heart: Prayers in the Old Testament were always spontaneous, personal, from the heart, in touch with actual reality, and were never repetitive.[271] In complete contrast, the Sages produced a fixed prayer book (סידור התפילה), mandatory for everyone, everywhere, and suitable for any occasion. They also made it mandatory to pray in public (מניין)[272] and only in a designated place, the synagogue.[273]

6. Elevating the Talmud at the Expense of the Bible: As mentioned earlier, the Sages argued that the Mosaic Covenant was based on the Oral Law.[274] They also declared that learning the Oral Law grants greater merit than studying the Bible.[275] And as if that is not enough, they argued that their authority is greater than the

---

[270]Amnon Shapira, 209.

[271]See: Hananel Mack, in Hebrew:
חננאל מאק, תפילה ותפילות, הוצאת ראובן מס בע"מ, ירושלים, 2008, עמ' 9-10, 80
And also: Zechariah Goren and Miriam Dror, 79.

[272]b. Talmud, Brachot 6b.

[273]Ibid., 6a, 8a. See further dissuasion in: Hananel Mack, 13-18.

[274]b. Talmud, Gittin 60b.

[275]j. Talmud, Pea 13b. Rabbi Yuval Sharlo admits that among the yeshivas today, studying the Bible is secondary to learning the Oral-Law; and even when the Tanakh is being studied, it's done only through the lenses of the traditional commentators. In: Bin-Nun, Yoel (in Hebrew):
הרב יובל שרלו, בתוך: יואל בן-נון, פרקי האבות: עיונים בפרשיות האבות בספר בראשית, בהוצאת: תבונות, 2003, 7-10

prophets in the Bible.[276]

7. Reducing God to a Yeshiva Student and Inevitably Bringing About His Defeat:[277] First, the Sages argue that God puts on phylacteries (תפילין) and prays every day for three hours.[278] Then, they claim that God is studying Talmud in heaven (and even quotes Rabbi Eliezer as an halachic authority).[279] And as if that were not enough, they also quoted God as saying, "my sons have defeated me, my sons have defeated me" (נצחוני בני, נצחוני בני), after He allegedly lost the argument in a ground breaking dispute over a certain oven.[280]

8. Crowning the Rabbis as Kings at the Expense of God: the Babylonian Talmud (Psachim 22b) says that a certain rabbi (named in Hebrew: נחמיה העמסוני) was learning the Torah; when he came to Deuteronomy 10:20, his disciples waited to hear his interpretation. This rabbi believed that the true meaning of the verse requires him to say that you must fear the Sages as you fear God, but he could not bring himself to make such a bold claim. Then Rabbi Akiva came and said: "Thou shalt fear the Lord thy God, and also the Sages"![281] From then on, the rabbis did not shy away from comparing their status to

---

[276]j. Talmud, Sanhedrin 55b.

[277]See further discussion in: Gruber, Daniel, 174–75.

[278]b. Talmud, Brachot 6a, 7a.

[279]Midrash B'Midbar Rabba, portion 19 (במדבר רבה, סדר חקת, פרשה י"ט).

[280]b. Talmud, Baba Metzia 59b.

[281]In Hebrew:
נחמיה העמסוני היה דורש כל אתים שבתורה. כיון שהגיע (דברים י) ל'את ה' אלהיך תירא', פירש. אמרו לו תלמידיו: רבי, כל אתים שדרשת מה תהא עליהן? אמר להם: כשם שקבלתי שכר על הדרישה כך אני מקבל שכר על הפרישה. עד שבא רבי עקיבא ודרש: את ה' אלהיך תירא, לרבות תלמידי חכמים

> God's status.[282] They saw themselves as the new kings of the earth,[283] and even started calling each other "kings" and treating themselves as such. The Babylonian Talmud records several examples of rabbis using the term "king" when greeting one another, and calling the head of the yeshiva "king."[284]

The rabbinic revolution was completed during the times of the Tannaim and their successors, the Amoraim (between the second and fifth century AD). The Sages abolished the validity of prophecy, of the Holy Spirit and of the voice from heaven (בת-קול). Moreover, they denied any interference of God in the new religion they had created. They used the Bible merely as an infrastructure out of which they could excuse whatever decree they wished to implement.[285] As mentioned, the Sages reinvented biblical prayer and, in fact, replaced it with mere recitations, which only they authorised. Thus, Judaism was made into a legal religion, full of rules, regulations and symbols, but without any intervention of the prophetic voice of God and His divine Spirit.[286] God and His living Word were pushed aside, the Sages could do without Him. He was no longer necessary,[287] and the traditions of the Oral Law, governed by the rabbis, took center stage.[288]

---

[282]Mishnah, Avot 4:15 (see also in: B. Talmud, Psachim 108a).

[283]See in: Steinsaltz, Adin, 26.

[284]Tur-Sinai, Naftali, Hertz, 391.

[285]Gruber, Daniel, 221, 233, 434–35.

[286]Hartman, David (in Hebrew):
דוד הרטמן, מסיני לציון: התחדשותה של ברית, בהוצאת: עם עובד, רעננה, 1992, עמ' 47-48

[287]Gruber, Daniel, 436.

[288]See: Aminoff, Irit (in Hebrew):

Hence, the atheistic reformation of the rabbis was twofold.[289] On the one hand, they denied the spirit and the essence of the Jewish faith, as reflected in the Bible; on the other hand, they pushed out Judaism's legitimate gatekeepers (i.e., the priests) and instead, turned themselves into authoritative human idols, to which all Israel must submit, obey, and even worship.[290]

עירית אמינוף, אבנים טובות ומיני סדקית: עיונים בתלמוד ובמדרש, הוצאת ראובן מס בע"מ, ירושלים, 2011, עמ' 103-106

[289]See: Lobkowitz, Iohannes C. (in Hebrew):
יוהנס קרמואל לובקוביץ, על האתאיזם של הרבנים, תרגום מלטינית: מרסל דיבואה, אביטל וולמן, יוסף שוורץ, בהוצאת י"ל מאגנס, ירושלים, 2005, עמ' 44

[290]See examples for this in the Mishnah, Avot 1:4, 2:13; and more contemporary ones in: Benjamin Lau, in Hebrew:
בנימין לאו, ממרן עד מרן: משנתו ההלכתית של הרב עובדיה יוסף, בהוצאת: משכל (ידיעות ספרים), 2005, עמ' 227-228

Chapter 10

THE MYTH OF THE ORAL LAW

This chapter will provide thirteen specific evidences which support the claim that the Oral Law was not a divine tradition given by Moses at Sinai.

1. The terms: "oral law" and "rabbis" are completely absent from the Tanakh.[291] In fact, the Talmud itself admits that Moses did not recognize the teaching of the Oral Law, when he allegedly heard Rabbi Akiva say at his yeshiva that the Oral Law he was teaching came straight from Moses himself, at Sinai.[292]

2. There is not even a hint of the Oral Law rulings in the Written Law.[293]

3. There is no scriptural record of any biblical figure practicing the rules of the Oral Law (not even putting on the phylacteries, which is considered by the rabbis to be one of the most important commandment of the Oral

[291]Even though the rabbis insist that the Written Law is the basis for the Oral Law (see for example, in: b. Talmud, Menachot 29b).

[292]Ibid.

[293]For example, nowhere in the Torah we find hints for the rabbinic laws concerning prayer, regarding kosher regulations, concerning the instructions for setting a mezuzah, etc. These are all later traditions, which the rabbis made mandatory.

Law[294]).

4. Scripture makes it perfectly clear, and in fact emphasizes, that the entire Torah was written down, so that it could be read aloud publicly (e.g., Exod 24:4, 12; 34:27, Deut 17:18–19, 31:24, Josh 8:32–35; 23:6; 24:26; 2 Kings 14:6; 22:8–13; Ezra 6:18; Neh 8:1–3, 13–18).

5. The Oral Law has many quotations from the Bible, but the Bible never quotes the Mishnah or any other rabbinic literature. This proves that the Oral Law came into existence much later than the Written Law and was not given on Sinai, as the rabbis claim.[295]

6. Many of the Oral Law rulings, customs, and traditions contradict the Bible, as we have shown earlier.

7. The Oral Law contradicts many scientific facts, proving it did not originate with God. Here are five examples:

    a) According to the Babylonian Talmud (Bechorot 8a), the gestation period of the snake is seven years. Scientifically, the female snake's pregnancy lasts less than a year.

    b) According to the Babylonian Talmud (Shabbat 107b), lice are not created as a result of mating but from human sweat. Scientifically, the lice

[294]See, for example: b. Talmud, Kiddushin, 35a; Psachim 113b.

[295]See, for example: Berel Wein, *Vision & Valor: An Illustrated History of the Talmud* (Jerusalem: Maggid books, 2010), 1, 10.

are a type of parasites, which are created by mating, like all other living creatures.

c) According to the Babylonian Talmud (Chulin 45b), the trachea divides into three brunches: one leads to the lung, one to the liver, and one to the heart. Anatomically, the trachea divides into two: one leads to the left lung, and the other to the right lung.

d) According to the Mishnah (Ohalot 1:9), there are eleven ribs on each side of the human body. Physiologically, there are actually twelve ribs on each side.

e) According to the Babylonian Talmud (Ketubot 39a), a pregnant woman can conceive again during her pregnancy. Physiologically, during pregnancy, a woman does not ovulate, and therefore no additional pregnancy is possible at that time.

8. The Talmud itself, not to mention the rest of the Oral Law, is loaded with many inner contradictions, and in fact, contradictions, arguments, and disputes are its hallmark.[296] This proves the Talmud did not have a single divine origin but rather portrays several opposing traditions. Here are five examples:

a) The Babylonian Talmud (Baba Kama 71a)

---

[296] Ronen Neuwirth, "Transcending Times" (in Hebrew):
רונן נויבירט, לגעת בזמן: החגים כחוויה בעולם המדרש, בהוצאת: משכל (ידיעות ספרים), 2016, עמ' 152
And also: Moshe Averbach, 130.

records a dispute between Rabbi Meir, Rabbi Judah, and Rabbi Yochanan over food that was cooked for the Sabbath.[297]

b) The Babylonian Talmud (Brachot 27b) records a controversy over the question of whether the evening prayer (תפילת ערבית) is mandatory or not? Rabbi Gamliel argued that it was mandatory (חובה). Rabbi Joshua said that it was not mandatory (רשות).

c) The Babylonian Talmud (Zevachim 29a) records a fundamental dispute between Rabbi Eliezer and Rabbi Akiva regarding the legitimacy of a specific sacrifice mentioned in Leviticus 7:16–18.[298]

d) The Babylonian Talmud (Yevamot 46a-b) records a controversy over the proper requirements for conversion. Rabbi Eliezer argued that circumcision is necessary, but not immersion. Rabbi Joshua argued that immersion is necessary, but not circumcision.

e) The Babylonian Talmud (Baba Batra 15a) records a dispute over the true author of Deuteronomy 34:5–12. One opinion is that Joshua wrote it. And the opposing claim argues

---

[297] Benjamin Lau, "Sages," vol 4: "From Mishnah to Talmud" (in Hebrew):
בנימין לאו, חכמים - כרך רביעי: ממשנה לתלמוד, בהוצאת: משכל (ידיעות ספרים), 2012, עמ' 224

[298] Shalom Rosenberg, in, Avinoam Rosenak, ed., in Hebrew:
שלום רוזנברג, בתוך: אבינועם רוזנק (עורך), הלכה, מטה-הלכה ופילוסופיה: עיון רב-תחומי, מכון ון ליר בירושלים
והוצאת מאגנס, 2011, עמ' 255-256

that Moses himself wrote it.

9. Even though the Torah forbids taking away or adding to its laws, the Sages have abolished many of the commandments and added countless new regulations which have nothing to do with the Written Law.

10. There is no mention of the Oral Law in the apocrypha, in the Septuagint, in the Dead Sea Scrolls, or in Josephus' writings.

11. The Ethiopian Jews (called also, "Beta-Israel") are a living proof that the advent of the Oral Law took place after the end of the Second Temple Period. These Jews, who kept a strict religious lifestyle for over two millennia, knew nothing about the Oral Law, because they had gone into exile long before the Sages ever came up with their traditions.[299]

12. Neither the Sadducees (צדוקים) nor the Karaites (קראים)[300] accepted the authoritative divine nature of the Oral Law, and therefore did not follow its traditions.[301] Some Karaites even argued that the Oral Law stands in direct opposition to God, and that it has kept the Jewish people away from the authentic Torah

[299] See: Michael Corinaldi, *Ethiopian Jewry: Identity and Tradition* (in Hebrew):
מיכאל קורינאלדי, יהדות אתיופיה: זהות ומסורת, הוצאת ראובן מס בע"מ, ירושלים, 2005, עמ' 62-64, 88-89, 116-117, 121
And also: Sharon Shalom, 11, 108.

[300] The Karaites probably began as a distinct Jewish movement around the 8th century A.D. See: Yoram Erder, *The Karaite Mourners of Zion and the Qumran Scrolls* (in Hebrew):
יורם ארדר, אבלי ציון הקראים ומגילות קומראן: לתולדות חלופה ליהדות הרבנית, בהוצאת: הקיבוץ המאוחד, רעננה, 2004, עמ' 38

[301] Ibid., 29, 45, 53, 120-122.

of Moses.[302]

13. Recent archeological findings, dating back towards the end of the Second Temple Period, of Jews who were exiled to Babylon, reveal that these Jews show no apparent familiarity with any Oral Law traditions. Rather, their Jewish identity was carried inwardly, with no external features resembling rabbinical practices.[303]

[302] Yoram Erder, *Methods in Early Karaite Halakha* (in Hebrew):
יורם ארדר, דרכים בהלכה הקראית הקדומה, בהוצאת: הקיבוץ המאוחד, רעננה, 2012, עמ' 11-17
See also: Nathan Shur, *The History of the Karaites* (in Hebrew):
נתן שור, תולדות הקראים, בהוצאת: מוסד ביאליק, ירושלים, 2003, עמ' 15-18

[303] See words of Yehuda Kaplan (יהודה קפלן, מנהל מחלקת חינוך והדרכה במוזיאון ארצות המקרא בירושלים); and Erving Finkel (ארווינג פינקל, אוצר במוזיאון הלאומי הבריטי), As revealed in the news media in Israel (in Hebrew), at: http://www.nrg.co.il/online/55/ART2/673/972.html and: http://www.ynet.co.il/articles/0,7340,L-4622368,00.html

Chapter 11

THE FOOTHOLD OF THE ORAL LAW TODAY

If the Pharisees had only six thousand members in the first century, now their descendants have an entire country supporting them, and millions of followers in Israel and worldwide. What started as a relatively small cult,[304] became a world religion, with considerable political power in the Jewish State of Israel.[305] Israel is legally a religious country (i.e., there is no separation between state and religion) and the religion in power is none other than the rabbinic one.[306]

Hence, the rabbis are being paid with taxpayer money to govern most of the country's institutions (e.g., army, food industry, Jewish holy sites, weddings, funerals, etc.). For example, every town and even many neighborhoods in Israel employ rabbis at full salary, who are primarily appointed to

---

[304] Uriel Rapoport, in: Menachem Stern, ed., 257.

[305]At least that is what they believe. See: Shahar Ilan, "Haredim LTD," in Hebrew:
אילן שחר, חרדים בע"מ: התקציבים, ההשתמטות ורמיסת החוק, כתר הוצאה לאור, ירושלים, 2000, עמ' 15-21

[306]See discussion at: Aviezer Ravitzky, In: Aviezer Ravitzky, ed., in Hebrew:
אביעזר רביצקי, בתוך: אביעזר רביצקי (עורך), דת ומדינה: בהגות היהודית במאה העשרים, בהוצאת: המכון הישראלי לדמוקרטיה, 2005, עמ' 9
And also: Gilli Zivan, in Aviezer Ravitzky, (ed.), in Hebrew:
גילי זיוון, בתוך: אביעזר רביצקי (עורך), שם, עמ' 431-442

conduct evening lessons in Talmud, but in fact, have wide ranging activities, at their initiative and discretion.[307]

No wonder, therefore, that Orthodox students, who spend all their time learning the Oral Law in yeshivas, are financially supported by the State to do just that.[308] In this sense, the revolution of the Oral Law has certainly paid off for the rabbis. They are not only considered the lawful gatekeepers of Israel and of the Jewish faith,[309] but they are also being supported and paid to do so directly by the State.[310]

Today, almost 50% of the population of Israel consider themselves to be religious or traditional to some degree (and well over 10% are ultra-orthodox).[311] This means that at least half of Israelis automatically identify rabbinic traditions with authentic Judaism. For them, and even for many secular Jews, to become religious or to serve God, means being obligated to the Oral Law. Thus, even though many groups and sects within rabbinical Judaism[312] demonstrate clear affinity with

---

[307] Asaph Midani, in: Yagil Levy, and Eti Sarig, eds., "The Local Government: Between the State, the Community and the Market Economy" (in Hebrew):
מידני, אסף, בתוך: יגיל לוי ואתי שריג (עורכים), השלטון המקומי - בין המדינה, הקהילה וכלכלת השוק: כרך א, בהוצאת: האוניברסיטה הפתוחה, רעננה, 2014, עמ' 199-198

[308]Ilan, Shahar, 185–202.

[309]Israel M. Lau, 11.

[310]See discussion in: Moshe Amar, In: Yoseph Hacker, and Yaron Harel, eds., in Hebrew:
משה עמאר, בתוך: יוסף הקר וירון הראל (עורכים), לא יסור שבט מיהודה: הנהגה, רבנות וקהילה בתולדות ישראל, בהוצאת: מוסד ביאליק, ירושלים, 2011, עמ' 385
And see also: Kimmy Caplan, in: Kimmy Caplan and Emmanuel Sivan eds., in Hebrew:
קימי קפלן, בתוך: קימי קפלן ועמנואל סיון (עורכים), חרדים ישראלים: השתלבות בלא טמיעה?, בהוצאת: מכון ון ליר בירושלים, הקיבוץ המאוחד, 2003, עמ' 239-234

[311] Haim Zicherman, "Black Blue-White: A Journey into the Charedi Society in Israel," in Hebrew:
חיים זיכרמן, שחור כחול לבן: מסע אל תוך החברה החרדית בישראל, בהוצאת: משכל (ידיעות ספרים), 2014, עמ' 344

[312]Ibid., 21. See also: Benjamin Brown, "Trembling at the Word of the People: Haredi Critique of Israeli Democracy," in Hebrew:
בנימין בראון, חרדים מ"שלטון העם": ביקורת חרדית על הדמוקרטיה הישראלית, בהוצאת: המכון הישראלי לדמוקרטיה, 2012, עמ' 48-33

cults,[313] most Jews would still recognize them as legitimate expressions of a continuance of biblical faith and as synonymous with true Judaism.

---

[313]See: Menachem Friedman, "The Haredi (Ultra-Orthodox) Society: Sources, Trends and Processes, in Hebrew:
מנחם פרידמן, החברה החרדית – מקורות, מגמות ותהליכים, בהוצאת: מכון ירושלים לחקר ישראל, 1991, עמ' 3, 144-149
And also: Amnon Levy, "The Ultra-Orthodox," in Hebrew:
אמנון לוי, החרדים, כתר הוצאה לאור, ירושלים, 1988, עמ' 145

Chapter 12

CONCLUSION: THE ORAL LIE

A specter has been haunting the Jewish world for over two millennia—the specter of rabbinic authority; a man-made religion which has developed its own particular system of laws, distinct and separate from the Bible—one which has placed its shackles of legalism on the Jewish people, at least since the destruction of the Second Temple.

This paper demonstrates when and how the Pharisees came into existence, what the historical and geo-political circumstances were, which paved the way for this group to push aside other competing parties, through developing the right connections at the highest political levels. This paper also demonstrates how a relatively small, but powerful, sect managed to impose its traditions and ideology upon the entire nation through the development and elevation of the Oral Law into a divine system which allegedly came straight from God.

This work shows how the rabbis have literally replaced the importance and authority of the Written Law with their Oral Law traditions and writings; The Sages carried out their revolutionary vision by addressing three fronts, or pillars, of the Jewish world and by reforming them completely: the priests were replaced with rabbis, the Temple was replaced with the yeshiva and the Bible was subordinated to the Oral Law teachings. We demonstrated why the Oral Law could not have originated with God, by presenting biblical, historical, and scientific evidences.

This paper also shows the pagan and Hellenistic influences, which were deliberately adopted by the Sages, in order to fill up the void made by the abandonment of authentic, biblical Judaism. Finally, we demonstrated how, after two thousand years, the rabbinic reformation reached its peak. Their traditions have become a state religion. So now, the rabbis are receiving the sponsorship of the State of Israel, while continuing to expand their influence throughout the Jewish world.

According to rabbinic literature, the Oral Law symbolizes the tree of knowledge:

> תורה שבעל פה שהיא עץ לדעת ונקראת עץ הדעת, קיומה בדעת שהוא הפה[314]

Meaning: "The Oral Law is a tree for knowledge and is called the tree of knowledge, its existence is in knowledge which is the mouth." Hence, studying the Oral Law resembles eating from the Tree of Knowledge, which, as written in Genesis 2:17, results in death. Sad to say, but for two thousand years and more, countless number of Jews devote their time to "eating" from this "Tree of Knowledge," while diligently studying the Talmud, day in and day out. We end this work

---

[314]Rabbi Meir Ben-Gabbai (b. 15th century AD). *Sefer Avodat HaKodesh* (in Hebrew):
רבי מאיר אבן גבאי, ספר עבודת הקודש, ירושלים, 1973, חלק א' פרק כ"ב

therefore, with a prayer that by the grace of God, their hearts would turn, and at last they will recognize—and taste of—the genuine Tree of Life. Amen!

HELP US GET THE SECRET OUT!

If this book was a blessing to you in any way, please leave a positive rating and review at this page on Amazon (goodreads.com will also be great) *as the rabbis will try to flood the review section with negative comments to discourage people from reading it.*

It would also be a great blessing if you can SHARE the link to this book on your social media profile, to help get the truth out.

Thank you!
Eitan Bar and Golan Broshi

English Bibliography

Brown, M. L. *Traditional Jewish Objections*. Vol. 5 of *Answering Jewish Objections to Jesus*. 5ed. Purple Pomegranate Productions, 2010.

Gruber, D., *Rabbi Akiba's Messiah: The Origins of Rabbinic Authority*. Tel Aviv: Maoz Israel, 2004.

Harari, Y. *The Sages and the Occult, in: Schwartz, J., Tomson, P. J., Safrai, S. & Safrai, Z. (eds.). The Literature of the Sages, Second Part*: Fortress Press, 2007, pp. 521-564.

Howland, J. *Plato and the Talmud*: Cambridge University Press, 2010.

Prof. Brown, B. Interviewed in "Israel Hayom" (ישראל היום). Weekend Edition, 2017, 29 Sept, p. 28.

Rabbi, Cecile. *Encyclopaedia Judaica.* 13ed. "P-REC." Jerusalem: Keter Publishing House, 1972.

Rabbi, Cecile. *Encyclopaedia Judaica.* 14ed. "RED-SL." Jerusalem: Keter Publishing House, 1972.

Rabbi, Cecile. *Encyclopaedia Judaica.* 15ed. "SM-UN." Jerusalem: Keter Publishing House, 1972.

Rabbi, Cecile. *Encyclopaedia Judaica.* 2ed. "A-ANG." Jerusalem: Keter Publishing House, 1972.

Rabbi, Cecile. *Encyclopaedia Judaica.* 8ed. "HE-IR." Jerusalem: Keter Publishing House, 1972.

Rabbi, Harvey. *Mapping Messianic Jewish Theology: A Constructive Approach.* Paternoster, 2009.

Rabbi, Joseph Telushkin. *Rebbe: The Life and Teachings of Menachem M. Schneerson, the Most Influential Rabbi in Modern History*. New York: HarperCollins Books, 2014.

Saks, J. *Educating Toward Meaningful Jewish Prayer*. Edited; Yoel Finkelman, Atid, 2001.

Schiffman, L. H. *From Text to Tradition: A History of Second Temple and Rabbinic Judaism*. 1ed. Ktav Pub Inc, 1991.

Stern, D. H. *Messianic Jewish Manifesto*. Jerusalem: Jewish New Testament Publications, 1988.

Hebrew Bibliography

.1998 ,©•®µ¥• ,©®µ ∂ú≤°† ,†•§¥≥™°∂°≤-•ú ,(¶¥ºÆ) ´••§µ¨••º Ƶ°†• :¶ºù ,.µ ,¥¨•ùú

.1973 ,©•®µ¥• ,µü≥† ∂ü°ùÆ¥∞≠ ,¥•ú™,•úùû´ùú

∂°Æü•) ®ßµ™:∂ú≤°†ù ,ú¥≥™† ®µ ∂•∞≠°®•∞†° ∂•§≠•™† ∂°¨µ¥∞ù :≥£≤• ∂ü≥Æ,.ú ,´£-´ùú .2006 ,(©•¥∞≠

.2008 ,©•®µ¥• ,™Æü ≠™ù°ú¥ ∂ú≤°† ,ü°™®∂†°†¨µ™† ∂∞≥∂ù •ü°†•† ¶°¨£† ,†µ™,¶ù¥ùú

,•ü°†•† ©Æ† ∂°ü®∂ ¥≥£®¥¢µ ™®¢ ¢ß¥™:∂ú≤°†ù ,ú•µ¨† †ü°†• •ù¥ ,´¥†ú ,¥™••†¨∞ú .2007 ,©•®µ¥•

.1976 ,≠¨ûú™®″• ∂ú≤°†ù ,∂°Æü°∂°¨°™ú •≥¥ßW ®′¢£ ,.ú .ú ,¶ù¥°ú

.2013 ,™§¥† ©®µ ´ß™:∂ú≤°†ù ,†ùµ£™∂°û† •¥ùü :£¥ •ùµ™,Ø≠• ,ù§•£ú

,´®ûù° ®•®ûù ∂≠¨ß-•∂ù - ®ú¥µ•±¥ú ∂Æü•®∂Æù∂ß :®ú•¥ú ,(¶¥ºÆ) ¥®•µ •®ú :¶ºù ,•ù≤ ,´®ú .1987 ,©•®µ¥• ,®ú•¥ú ©•¥∞≠ ∂ú≤°†

,†¨¨Æ¥ ,üù°Æ©Æ∂ú≤°†ù ,†ù°µ∂†°∂ü† ∂°¢£™ú ∂•¨∂ú°¥üû™:©•¥°™µ ∂°™≥™,¥™∞ ,¥°ú®ú .2006

.1999 ,´®•ú ¥ù ∂§•≠¥ù•¨°ú ∂ú≤°† ,ü°™®∂† •™ú •¥ùÆ† §∞µ™®ú°ù™,©°®µ ,≥ù®ú

.2011 ,(©•¥∞≠ ∂°Æü•) ®ßµ™:∂ú≤°†ù ,•ü ú™®Æ,•¥ú ,´°®ú

±°ù•≥† ,©•®µ¥•ù ¥•®´° ´ß™:∂ú≤°†ù ,†ü°†• ¥ùü™∂°®•ú™®µ ´ü≠ :†••µ¨° ´¥ß•¢ ,®£¥ ,¥°ú•®ú .2009 ,ü£°ú™†

¥ù ∂§•≠¥ù•¨°ú ∂ú≤°† ,©•∂°û†° ©•¥§≠•† ,©••∞¥ûú•û ©•¥≥£™:ú¥≥™†° ®ú¥µ• ,†ü°†• ,¥≤•®ú .2000 ,´®•ú

,™Æü ≠™´ù°ú¥ ∂ú≤°† ,µ¥ü™ú° ü°™®∂ù ©•¨•Æ:∂•≥ü≠ •¨•™ ∂°§ ©•¨ùú ,∂•¥•Æ,Ø¨•™ú .2011 ,©•®µ¥•

:∂ú≤°†ù ,∂•¨ù¥† ∂°†•® †∞®£ ∂°ü®∂® :´ú¥™≥ ∂°®•™ ©•ú¥≥† ´•≤ •®ùú ,©¥• ,¥ü¥ú .2004 ,†¨¨Æ¥ ,ü£°ú™† ±°ù•≥†

.2012 ,†¨¨Æ¥ ,ü£°ú™† ±°ù•≥† :∂ú≤°†ù ,†™ü≥† ∂•ú¥≥† †ß®†ù ©•ß¥ü ,©¥• ,¥ü¥ú

.2013 ,(©•¥∞≠ ∂°Æü•) ®ßµ™:∂ú≤°†ù ,†¢† ©•† üÆ,´°™ú ,≥¢ú

.1968 ,'°,´®•ú-¥ù ∂§•≠¥ù•¨ˆú ,©•ú˜µ≥ ∂Æ•§¨ ∂ßß®†°©•∞µß ∂ßß®† ,ù≥Æ,≥¢ù

.1962 ,ù•ùú-®∂ ,¥•ùü ∂ú≤°† ,†üûú† ¥∞≠ ,.•,•≥≤•¨ù¥°.£ ,≥•®ú•ù

.2011 ,´®•ú ¥ù ∂§•≠¥ù•¨ˆú ∂ú≤°† ,©•®ùú ©£•¨°©•®£ ¥°≥•ù :†¨ù••¥%∞≠ ,†•¥¢Æ,¥¨§•ù

©•¥∞≠† ∂ú≤°† ,®ú¥µ•ù •¨¥•Æ† ¥∞≠ù ©≥•ü≤° ∂ˆú∞¥™,©•™®£ :©•µˆü≥† •¨ùµˆµ ,©¥°• ,°®ù
.2005 ,†∞•£ ∂§•≠¥ù•¨ˆú ®µ

,†£%∂∞† †§•≠¥ù•¨ˆú† :†ú≤°†ù ,∂•£•µ™† ü"ù£ù •ù¥† ∂£ß¨† :ü•™∂™¥∂• °¨∂ú ,©¥°• ,°®ù
.2017 ,†¨¨Æ¥

†µ¥ü† ,´µ¥ü† :°™Æ®ù§ µ¥°ü ,(©•ß¥°Æ) ±•ù¥°† •™¥ß°´®•≥ •™≥ ,´®•ú ©£¨ :¶%ù ,•§°™¶®™ù
,©•®µ ¥• ,•ü°†•† ©Æ† ∂ˆü®∂ ¥≥£®¥¢µ ™®¢ ¢ß¥™:∂ú≤°†ù ,∂•ü°†•† ∂ˆù¥∂ù µ ¥ü† ∂¥∞≠°
.2012

´ß™† :∂ú≤°†ù ,∂•®ú¥µ•† †•§¥≥°™ü† ®Æ∂•ü¥£ ∂¥°≥•ù :"©Æ† ´§®µ"™©•ü¥£ ,´•™ù ,´ú¥ù
.2012 ,†•§¥≥°™ü®•®ú¥µ•†

,™Æü ≠™ùˆú¥ ∂ú≤°† ,†üûúù°µ¥ü™ü ú∂¥ù£ :¥°™ü †≤¥∂ ©ú°,®®† ü%ü ,¥¨•∞ •ü°™,•≥≤ü¥ù
.2007 ,©•®µ ¥•

•ü°†•† •™≤Æ† ´§®µ† :®ú¥µ• ®†≥ ,(©•ß¥°Æ) ´®•≥ Ø≠°• ™≠¥û ©†¥ùú :¶%ù ,•ßü¥™,¥ú•°¥ù
∂ˆü®∂ ¥≥£®¥¢µ ™®¢ ¢ß¥™:∂ú≤°†ù ,(ù ¶¥ß) ∂™ü≥°™† †µü£† ∂Æ†°©•¨•ù† •™- %∂¥ˆü®
.2004 ,©•®µ ¥• ,•ü°†•† ©Æ†

.2009 ,∂°¨ˆù∂ ∂ú≤°†ù ,∂ˆú¥≥™≥¥∞,•ßü¥™,¥ú•°¥ù

,´®•ú ¥ù ∂§•≠¥ù•¨ˆú ∂ú≤°† ,®¢£ ∂ùµ£™ü ∂°•ú¨≥ï•§¨ú ∂°™ü™:ü≠£®∂ˆú¨≥ ´•ù ,ü%ü ,≠•¢¥ù
.2015

•¥∞≠ ,∂°¨¥£ú ∂°Æü• ∂ú≤°†ù ,®ú¥µ• ©Æ∂ˆü®∂ ®µ •¥%≠••†† ≠®§ú† ,(¶¥°Æ) •®ú ,ú•ù¨-¥ù
.1993 ,ü™£

†ú%¥ù ∂°Æ™≥ - ®ú¥µ• ±¥ú ∂Æü•® ∂Æù∂ß :®ú•¥ú ,(©•ß¥°Æ) •®ú ,¥®µ° ®ú•¥ùû ,•ú≥¥ù
.2006 ,®ú•¥ú ©¥∞≠ ∂ú≤°† ,ùû¨ù ©•°üù† ù¥≥ù ∂•™™Æ†

.2009 ,©•®µ ¥• ,ú¥°™®•µ ©¥∞≠ ∂ú≤°† ,¶¥Æ£®µ ¥≤≥ ,†™®µ ,ü¥∞≤¨úû

,%≠£° ´•®Æ† ®•®û† :3 ¶¥ß - ®•§ •®®≠™,†•ü∞®≥•≤¨ú :µü£† ®ú¥µ•¶•¥ü™,(¶¥°Æ) ´µ°™,•úùû
.2001 ,´£§•ù† ü¥µ™,∂°¨¥£ú ∂°Æü• ,¥ˆú®†ú≤† ¥∂ß

.2000 ,†¨¨Æ¥ ,∂"∞°™ß™,(•§≥ü•ü ¶•¥ü™)†®∞∂† ¥ü•≠ ®Æ,©•¥™,¥¥ü°†•¥ß¢,¥ˆû

.1978 ,™Æü ©••™ü≥ú ©•™≠¥∞- ®≥ü ∂ú≤°† ,∂¨≥∂™†ú¥°†ù ©µü£ ©•§ù•† ,©•¥™,≠•®û

.1992 ,´®•ú ¥ù ∂§•≠¥ù•¨ˆú ∂ú≤°† ,†ß®†† ∂°®µ®∂µ†ù ©≥¥∞,'ü ≥£≤• ,∂®û

.1936 ,≥•®ú•ù ü≠°™∂ú≤°† ,∂•¥ûú •ù∂ß ,©••£ ,û¥ù¢¨û

.1921 ,´•®¥ù ,•µ•®µ ≥®£ ,'ù ¶¥ß ,©•ß¥ü ∂µ¥∞®Æ¶ª∂ù ,"£¥º¥µù" ,('©Æ‡ ü£ú') ûª≤ú ,û¥ù≤¨•û

ü≠ª™:∂ú≤ª†ù ,†¥ª∂® •"µ¥ µª¥•∞ù ∂ª¥ù£∂ ∂ª≠•∞∂ :´µ®ùßº ´µ¥∞ß •"µ¥ ,¶º¨£ ,®ú•®™ú
.2010 ,©•®µ ª¥• ,≥•®ú•ù

,ü£ªú™‡ ±ªù•≥† :∂ú≤ª†ù ,†µü£† ∂Æ•ü ®'¢£ ∂ª¥∞≠ ¥≥£ù ©•¨ªÆ'†¨µ™®µ †§ªµ∞ ,¨£ ,•¨∞û
.2011 ,†¨¨Æ¥

¥≥£®¥¢µ ™®¢ ¢ß¥™:∂ú≤ª†ù ,£ª¥†º †¥ù£† •£ :üª™®∂† ∂∞≥∂ù ®ùù •üª†• ,ª†•Æµ• ,•¨∞û
.1990 ,©•®µ ª¥• ,•üª†•† ©Æ‡ ∂ªü®∂

±ªù•≥† :∂ú≤ª†ù ,∂•üª†•† ∂¥ª≠™ú ∂ª•®ú≠≥≠ª™‡ :©•µ¨ú ©Æ ©•†ª®ú ©Æ,´ù•§≠ ,û¥ù¨¥û
.2013 ,†¨¨Æ¥ ,ü£ªú™‡

.2003 ,¥ªú®†ú≤ª†º•ª∞•™W †∞ª™∂ú≤ª†ù ,∂•üª†•† †•û®∂•™‡ ,•ü£ ,´üü

.2006 ,©•®µ ª¥• ,•üª†•† ©Æ‡ ∂ªü®∂ ¥≥£®¥¢µ ™®¢ ¢ß¥™:∂ú≤ª†ù ,ü•≠£† †üª†•'¥ ,Ø≠ª• ,´ü

.2010 ,†¨¨Æ¥ ,ü£ªú™‡ ±ªù•≥† :∂ú≤ª†ù ,®ú¥µ•ù ©µü≥™©≤Æ,±ª™ú ,•¨∞ü

.1975 ,ù•ùú ®∂ ,©•¨•§ú®©•¨ª•∂ª¥≥™¥ªú®,∂•∞¥ûª•ù-∂•¥ª§≠†† †üûú† ,¶®™®ú ,•ª®‡

70) •§¨¢•ù† ´§®µ†ºüª™®∂†º†¨µ™‡ ∂∞≥∂ - ®ú¥µ•-±¥ú ®µ †•¥ª§≠•†† ,(¶¥ºÆ) üªü †µ™¥†
.1985 ,©•®µ ª¥• ,¥ªú®†ú≤ª† ¥∂ß •ù≤-´ù ≥£≤• ü• ,(640-

.1992 ,†¨¨Æ¥ ,üùºÆ©Æ:∂ú≤ª†ù ,∂•¥ù ®µ †∂ªµü£∂† :ª•≤®•¨•≠™,üªü ,™§¥†

•™•ú≤ª™üÆ†¥ª≤† •ª¨•µº•¨µ ∂•ù •™Ø≠ üÆµªù•û† •ß•®†∂ :∂•ú¥≥™‡ †∞ª≠ú† ,©£¨™,¥†
.1996 ,≠¨ûú™®'• ,©•®µ ª¥•ù ∂•¥ùÆ‡ †§•≠¥ù•¨ªú† ,≥•®ú•ù ü≠ª™,ú ≥®£ - ©•¨•ù†

•™•ú≤ª™üÆ†¥ª≤† •ª¨•µº•¨µ ∂•ù •™Ø≠ üÆµªù•û† •ß•®†∂ :∂•ú¥≥™‡ †∞ª≠ú† ,©£¨™,¥†
.2003 ,≠¨ûú™®'• ,©•®µ ª¥•ù ∂•¥ùÆ‡ †§•≠¥ù•¨ªú† ,≥•®ú•ù ü≠ª™∂ú≤ª†ù ,ù ≥®£ - ©•¨•ù†

.2014 ,(©¥∞≠ ∂ºÆüü•) ®ßµ™∂ú≤ª†ù ,∂•üª™®∂† †™µ¨† ,•®ú ,®¢•º

±ªù•≥† ∂ú≤ª†ù ,®'¢£ ∂ª¥∞≠ù ∂ªüºÆ≠† ®µ •∂ªù¥∂† ´ü•≥∞∂ :∂Æü® ©•®ßªú ,†™£¥ ,≠•ª•º
.2010 ,ü£ªú™‡

,™Æü ¥ªú®†ú≤ª† ©•™‡ •¥ùü ,©¥ùüW ¶"¨∂† ©®ºÆ,(©•ß¥ºÆ) üªü £™≤-´†ßº †µ™,ü®∞¨•º
.2002 '™Æ, ,†¨¨Æ¥

∂¥ª∞•≠ù ©•¥≥£™- ¥ª∞•≠ †µÆ™,(©•ß¥ºÆ) •≥≠ù®µº≥ †®¥º ¥≥≠∞®ùüü•ùú :¶ª∂ù ,®®† ,≠•º
.2006 ,´®ú ¥ù ∂§•≠¥ù•¨ªü ∂ú≤ª† ,∂•üª†•†

,≥•®ú•ù ü≠ª™:∂ú≤ª†ù ,´ú¥™≥ ∂ª®•û™ú †ß®†º ∂º¨µ¥∞ :∂¥∂≠¨ ∂ª®ú®,.ú ,µ™µº .ß ,™¥º
.2011 ,©•®µ ª¥•

,©¥µÆ‡ †ú™ú ∂•üª†•† ∂ªû†ù :†¨•ü™∂ü ,(¶¥ºÆ) •≥≤•ù¥¥¢Æüú :¶ª∂ù ,¥¢Æüú ,•®û ,´ª•¢
.2005 ,†•§¥≥ª™ú®•®ú¥µ•† ´ß™‡ :∂ú≤ª†ù

[illegible] .2014

[illegible] .2010

[illegible] .1981

[illegible] .1955

[illegible] .1959

[illegible] .2016

[illegible] .2013

[illegible] .1997

[illegible] .2005

[illegible] .2008

[illegible] .2012

[illegible] .2008

[illegible] .2017

[illegible] .2005

[illegible] .1988

[illegible] .1996

[illegible] .1996

[illegible] .1989

[illegible] .1962

[illegible]

.1988 ,©•®µ¥• ,≥•®ú•ù ü≠ª™

,(©•¥∞≠ ∂ºÆ•ü•) ®ßµ™·∂ú≤ª†ù ,'† ∂üªùÆü ©•ß¥Æ∂ªü•™· ªß®†•¶•¨∞¥ªúù ,¥†ú ,´••§µ¨§ß•®
.2012

.1993 ,†¨¨Æ¥ ,´ª£§•ù† ü¥µ™·∂ú≤ª†ù ,ú¥≥™®†™ªü≥† ∂º¨µ¥∞† ,®ú¨¨£ ,≥ú™

,†ùªµ••º®ú¥µ•±¥ú ∂ªü®∂®∂Æùß :†¥ü∂≥ ,"†µª¥üü †¥ü∂≥º†µ™ªú †¥ü∂≥" ,®ú¨¨£ ,≥ú™
.1994 •¨ª ,72 ∂¥ùª£

.2008 ,©•®µ¥• ,™Æü ≠™ùªú¥ ∂ú≤ª† ,∂º®•∞∂º†®•∞∂ ,≥ú™®ú¨¨£

,†£∂®ªW üùß :ü - ª∂∞≥∂ºú¥≥™† ®µ ∂ºÆ•ü•† ¥≤ªú :∂•ú¥≥™†•ü∞®≥•≤ú ,(¶¥ºÆ) ´•™•ªù ,¥¢™
.1962 ,©•®µ¥• ,≥•®ú•ù ü≠ª™·∂ú≤ª†ù

,•¥∂≠W ´ßª™™·† - ª∂∞≥∂ºú¥≥™† ®µ ∂ºÆ•ü•† ¥≤ªú :∂•ú¥≥™†•ü∞®≥•≤ú ,(¶¥ºÆ) ´•™•ªù ,¥¢™
.1968 ,©•®µ¥• ,≥•®ú•ù ü≠ª™·∂ú≤ª†ù

,•¨∂∂W ©µ :£ - ª∂∞≥∂º ú¥≥™† ®µ ∂ºÆ•ü•† ¥≤ªú :∂•ú¥≥™†•ü∞®≥•≤ú ,(¶¥ºÆ) ´•™•ªù ,¥¢™
.1982 ,©•®µ¥• ,≥•®ú•ù ü≠ª™·∂ú≤ª†ù

∂®ß®ßº†®•†≥† ,†¨•ü™† ´•ù - •™≥™† ´§®µ† ,(©•ß¥ºÆ) û•¥µ •∂úº•®®û• :¶ª∂ù ,Ø≠ú ,•¨ü•™
.2014 ,†¨¨Æ¥ ,†£ª∂∞† †§•≠¥ù•¨ªú† :∂ú≤ª†ù ,ú ¶¥ß :≥ªµ†

,®ú¥µ• ±¥úù ©≥•ü≤ •¥ù≥º ©•µªü≥ ∂ª™≥™,†µ™,¥¨®ª™ †üª†• ,´ª™®≠ ,©£¨™,´≠®ß•™
.2000 ,´ª£§•ù† ü¥µ™·∂ú≤ª†ù

∂•µª™µ †•ü∞®≥•≤ú :®ú¥µ•±¥ú ®µ £™≤†º•£† ,(©•ß¥ºÆ) ©¥ª• ,ùª§ ©•º ¶•¥¨••† ,´≠®ú¨™
.1988 ,†¨¨Æ¥ ,´ª£§•ù† ü¥µ™·∂ú≤´†ù ,©≥¨W 7 ¶¥ß - ∂¥••ªú™

∂º¨µü£º∂ªû† - ∂º¨ß∞†™,∂•¥≥™,∂º¥™µ :©ªù™¥† ,(¶¥ºÆ) •≥≤•ù¥ ¥¢Æ•ùú :¶ª∂ù ,.ù ,´≥¨™
.2009 ,©•®µ¥• ,•üª†•† ©Æ† ∂ªü®∂ ¥≥£®¥¢µ ™®¢ ¢ß¥™·∂ú≤ª†ù ,(ù ¶¥ß)

.2014 ,ü™£ •¥∞≠º∂º¨¥£ú ∂ºÆ•ü• :∂ú≤ª†ù ,∂ªü†•† ®µ ©•®üû©•£ß•º 10W ≥•∂ ,©••£ ,´ªü¨

.2008 ,©•®µ¥• ,™Æü ≠™ùªú¥ ∂ú≤ª† ,ù•ú ¥∞≠ù ´•Æü™®:¥µ•º©∂ µ•ú ,ª†•Æµ• ,®≤ªü¨

.2016 ,(©•¥∞≠ ∂ºÆ•ü•) ®ßµ™·∂ú≤ª†ù ,µ¥ü™† ©®Æü †•ª£ß ©•û£† :™¥ù ∂Æü®,˜¨¥ ,§¥•ù•º

ü• :∂ú≤ª† ,´µú¥ ¶¥ß - ©•¥≥£™∂ªúªù™´ú¥™≥ ∂º®•û™,(¶¥ºÆ) ¥§≠•≥ ©£¨™·¶ª∂ù ,.ù ,´≤•¨
.2009 ,©•®µ¥• ,•ù≤´ù ≥£≤•

,∂ªù¥∂†º †¥ù£† ∂ªü®∂ù ©≥¥∞ :†¨µ™† ∂∞≥∂ùº •¨µ† ∂•ù† •†®µù ,®ú™µ ,•ú¥∞≠
.1983 ,©•®µ¥• ,®ú¥µ••üª†•† ©Æ† ∂ªü®∂ ¥≥£®¥¢µ ™®¢ ¢ß¥™·∂ú≤ª†ù

1993- ,†¨¨Æ¥ ,™Æü ¥ªú®†ú≤ª† ©•™† •¥ùü ,'ù ©•®†∂ - ¶"¨∂† ©®Æ,(¶¥ºÆ) .™©£¨ ,†¨¥≠
.1996

.2012 ,†¨¨Æ¥ ,üùºÆ©Æ∂ú≤ª†ù ,´úß µ£¥∂† †™;®úû• ,©®•Æ

†®†≥° ∂°˙ù¥ ,†ûñ¨† :†ü°†•™§ùµ ¥≠• ú®,(©ß¥°Æ) ®ú¥† ´¥•°¥≥† Ø≠• :¶°∂ù ,†µ™¥ú™Æ
.2011 ,©•®µ ¥• ,≥•®ú•ù ü≠°™∂ú≤°†ù ,®ú¥µ• ∂°ü®°∂ù

,('†ú°µ'†) †"µ∂-µ"∂ ∂°¥ûù° ∂°™£®™ •∂µ ´•ù ∂•°•Æ¥ ∂°™™´•®∞ ∂°ü•≠£ ,®ù¨™'¢ú≥•∞
.1990 ,©•®µ ¥• ,≥•®ú•ù ü≠°™∂ú≤°†ù

,†¨¨Æ¥ ,ü£°ú™ ±°ù•≥† :∂ú≤°†ù ,†®ßµ†† ∂°ü†• ∂¥•≤•®≥ùú™ :†¨µ•®†¥§Æ,†µ™,•ú®∞
.2012

®µ †•¥°§≠•†† ,(©ß¥°Æ) .≤ ,≠¥ù° .™,†¨•-•ùú :¶°∂ù ,•¨µ ∂•ù ∂∞≥∂ù ®ú¥µ• ∂ü ,ü°ü ,¥≠°®∞
.1983 ,üù°Æ©Æ¥°ú®†ú≤°† ,©•®µ ¥• ,•¨µ ∂•ù •™ù ∂ü°†¥ù£ - ®ú¥µ• ©Æ

.1985 ,†¨¨Æ¥ ,´£§•ù† ü¥µ™∂ú≤°†ù ,©•≠•ú†°†ü°†•¥ùü™∂°®û™,ü°ü ,¥≠°®∞

.2002 ,©•®µ ¥• ,≠¨ûú™∂ú≤°† ,†∂°¥∞≠°†•™ß£ ,•¨µ ∂•ù ∂°ü†• ,ü°ü ,¥≠°®∞

∂ú≤°†® †¥ù£ ,†µ•™£° ©¥µÆ¶¥ß ,∂•¥ùÆ †•ü∞®≥•≤¨ú† ,(•µú¥ ¶¥°Æ) ,Æµ°†• ,¥°ú¥∞
.1974 ,™Æù ∂°ü∞®≥•≤¨ú

,∂°∂¥∞≠ ∂°û≠ ©≥¥™ù ∂°∂ß®† ∂°û≠ ®µ ´™≥™:†®ßµ†® †ß®† ´•ù ,†ü°†• ,¥ü¨®ù¥∞
.2004 ,´®ú ¥ù ∂§•≠¥ù•¨ú ∂ú≤°†ù

¥≥£® ©•®µ ¥• ´ß™:∂ú≤°†ù ,©ß•®†∂° ∂°™ù™,∂¥°≥™W ∂•ü¥£† †¥ù£† ,©£¨™,™ù•¥∞
.1991 ,®ú¥µ•

.1998 ,†¨•ü™ ´°ß¥ú :∂ú≤°†ù ,•¨µ† úµ¨† :•ù≤-´ù ≥£≤• ,(©ß¥°Æ) †™™,®§¨¢¥°•û£ ,Ø¥≤

.1950 ,≥•®ú•ù ü≠°™∂ú≤°† ,∂°ùú† ∂∞≥∂ù ©•¨Æß †®®Æ¥µ :∂¨Æ†®ú† ,.ü .™§≠ú≥

.2007 ,´û∂™¥ ,´®ú-¥ù ∂§•≠¥ù•¨ú ∂ú≤°†ù ,∂•ú¥≥™ ∂•¥ùÆ ´®™,≤.™•¥ü≥

.2005 ,©•®µ ¥• ,™Æù ≠™ù°ú¥ ∂ú≤°† ,∂¥≠™∂°†¢:†∞°∂ú ∂°ü†• ,•ü®ú¨¥≥ ®úß•™

,∂°¨ü∂ :∂ú≤°†ù ,¥ú•¥ù •ßü¥™ù¥† ®µ '∂°¨•£ù† ∂§•µ' ,(¶¥°Æ) ¥∞°ÆØ≠•:¶°∂ù ,•ù≤ ,®•∞≤¥≥
.2005

,•ù≤-´ù ≥£≤• ü• :∂ú≤°†ù ,´µú¥ ¶¥ß - ©•¥ùÆ ©¥°ù•£† :†ü°†• ¥ùü™∂°®û™,Æµ•®ú ,´¥™≥
.2010 ,©•®µ ¥•

±°ù•≥† :∂ú≤°†ù ,§≠•¨™†† ¶°•£ù ©™≤Æ™©û®ú•ü ,(¶¥°Æ) •¨®ú ü¥™ :¶°∂ù ,.¥ ,´¥ü®≥
.2008 ,†¨¨Æ¥ ,ü£°ú™

†•¥ù§W ®ú¥µ• ±¥ú ∂Æü•®∂Æù∂ß :®ú•¥ú ,(©ß¥°Æ) ¥®µ •®ú°¥û•ù ´Æû:¶°∂ù ,®ú¥µ• ,•£™≥
.1987 ,©•®µ ¥• ,®ú•¥ú ©¥∞≠ ∂ú≤°† ,†∂ù•ù≠°

.2016 ,™Æù ¥°ú®†ú≤°† ≠ü¥∞:∂ú≤°†ù ,©®Æù ¥ûñ™®¶¥ü :©≥™ ¥¥£µ ,´¥Æ,•£™≥

,ü£°ú™ ±°ù•≥† ∂ú≤°† ,©•¨ù† •™ù ∂•¨∞≤† †∞¥•úù ∂•ü°†•† †¥ù£†° ¶°•£† ,.ú ,®û∞¥≥
.2003 ,ù•ùú-®∂

,?†Æ•™§ ú®ù ∂ªù®®µ† :©•®ú¥µ• ©•ü¥£ ,(©•ß¥ºÆ) ´ª≠ ®ú°™Æ ´®≥ •™≥ :¶ª∂ù ,•™≥ ,´®≥
.2003 ,ü£ªú™ ±ªù•≥† ,©•®µ ¥•ù ¥•®´° ´ß™∂ú≤ª†ù

≠™´ùªú¥ ∂ú≤ª† ,Æ•ùµ† ∂ªµ¥∞ù° †¨µ† ®ûÆ™ªù ©•¨ªÆ¶®≥ ∂ú •¨•Æ™µ† ,(∂ß¥ºÆ) ®£¥ ,¥≥
.2009 ,©•®µ ¥• ,™Æû

.1969 ,©•®µ ¥• ,™Æû ≠™´ùªú¥ ∂ú≤ª† ,´µú¥¶¥ß ®ú¥µ• ∂ùµ£™ù ©•¨ªÆ ´ºÆ™µ ,±•ùªù•ùú¥

,©•¥µÆ† †ú™ù ∂•üª†•† ∂ªû†ù :†¨ü™ ∂ü ,(¶¥ºÆ) •≥≤ù¥ ¥¢Æùú :¶ª∂ù ,¥¢Æùú ,•≥≤ù¥
.2005 ,†•§¥≥ª™ù®•®ú¥µ•† ´ß™ :∂ú≤ª†ù

,•™£∂-ù¥ ´ªÆ:†•∞≠ª®•∞ †ß®†-†§™,†ß®† ,(¶¥ºÆ) ≥¨¢¥ ©Æ¨•ùú :¶ª∂ù ,¥¢Æùú ,•≥≤ù¥
.2011 ,©•®µ ¥• ,∂•¥ùÆ† †§•≠¥ù•¨ªú† ,≠¨ûú™∂ú≤ª†ù

,©•®µ ¥• ,•ù≤-´ù ≥£≤• ü• :∂ú≤ª†ù ,•¨µ ∂•ù •™ù †¥ù£° ∂ü ®Æ:©∂ß®†° ©•≥ªü≤† ,®ú ,ùû¥
.2005

.2005 ,†¨¨Æ¥ ,ü£ªú™ ±ªù•≥† :∂ú≤ª†ù ,©••£† ∂•µú¥ ,´≠•¨ ,´•ù¥

.1997 ,∂°ªù∂ :∂ú≤ª†ù ,µªù•£°∂¥≠™ †∞®Æùµ †¥ª∂ :ú•† ©•™µù ú®,©®µ ,û¥ù¨¢¥

´°´ß™,•™£∂-ù¥ ´ªÆ:†•∞≠ª®•∞ †ß®†-†§™,†ß®† ,(¶¥ºÆ) ≥¨¢¥ ©Æ¨•ùú :¶ª∂ù ,©®µ ,û¥ù¨¢¥
.2011 ,≠¨ûú™∂ú≤ª†° ©•®µ ¥•ù ¥•®

.2007 ,™Æû ©¥∞≠ ¥∂ß :∂ú≤ª†ù ,•®ú¥µ•† ù£¥™ù ∂ªµ :©••£† ®µ ´≥•≠≥®† ,≥•ù¥ ,®§¨¢¥

•™ù ∂ªü†•° ©•üª†• ,(©•ß¥ºÆ) ,¥™•†¨∞ú ¥†ú° •¨∞ûª†•Æµ• ,¥§µ ©£¨™¶ª∂ù ,´ª≤-´ù ,ü®∞¢¥
.1993 ,©•®µ ¥• ,•ù≤-´ù ≥£≤• ü• :∂ú≤ª†ù ,üª™®∂†°†¨µ™ ,•¨µ ∂•ù

,©•®µ ¥•ù ¥•®´° ´ß™∂ú≤ª†ù ,†¥ù£° ∂ªù¥∂ ,∂ªû† :∂•™¥∞¥† ∂ªü†•† ,(¶¥ºÆ) ©Æ¨•ùú ,≥¨¢¥
.2014 ,ü£ªú™ ±ªù•≥†

.2013 ,†¨¨Æ¥ ,ü£ªú™ ±ªù•≥† :∂ú≤ª†ù ,∂•¨ú™ † •≠≥ªù∂¥ªú ,¥•ú™§¥

.1985 ,†¨¨Æ¥ ,©•®Æ∞∂•¥∞≠ :∂ú≤ª†ù ,®¢£ ®µ †•ûûü∞:©®ß üû¨ß ,.ú .ú ,´•®ù•¥

,ü•™®∂® ,§¨ü§≠® ,´••Æ™®- û£® ∂ùµ® ∂•µª™µ †•ü∞®≥≤ú :®ú¥µ• •üÆ™ ,®úª ,®¥
.1990 ,†¨¨Æ¥ ,´£§•ù† ü¥µ™∂ú≤ª†ù

∂¨•ü™∂•§≠•¨®†† †∞≥∂¥V ®ú¥µ•±¥ú ®µ †•¥§≠••†† ,(¶¥ºÆ) ,¥§µ ©£¨™¶ª∂ù ,.ú ,§¥ª∞¥
.1981 ,©•®µ ¥• ,¥ªú®†ú≤ª† ¥∂ß ,•ù≤-´ù ≥£≤• ü• ,(†¥∞≠† •¨∞®37 - 332) ©•ú¨ª™µ£†

∂ºÆü•) ®ßµ™∂ú≤ª†ù ,©••ù† •™ù ∂•üª†•† †•∞≠ª®•∞† :º®µ ©•®ûûª† ©•∞≠ª®•∞† ,.ú ,ü•ùµ
.2009 ,(©¥∞≠

.1972 ,©•®µ ¥• ,≥•®ú•ù ü≠ª™∂ú≤ª†ù ,©•¥™ù™¥ªµ ®•µ† Æµª†• ,(¶¥ºÆ) ®•µ† Æµª†• ,¥ªµ

.2003 ,©•®µ ¥• ,≥•®ú•ù ü≠ª™∂ú≤ª†ù ,©•ú¥≥† ∂ªü®∂ ,´∂¨ ,¥ªµ

.2002 ,´®ú ¥ù ∂§•≠¥ù•¨ªú ∂ú≤ª† ,©••ù† •™ù ∂•üª†•† ∂ªû†ù †¥∂≠†°†¥•∂≠ ,ùü ,±¥ªµ

.2010 ,´®•ú ¥ù ∂§•≠¥ù•¨ú ∂ú≤ª†ù ,∂•¥£ú üÆ∂•µú¥™ü"ù£ ∂ùµ£™ùü ,±¥ªµ

∂ªµ¥∞ ,©•™ß•≠ ,∂¥≥™:ª∂∞≥∂° ≠ªü¥ª† ¶®™ ,(¶¥°Æ) ¥ú¨ •ßü¥™:¶ª∂ù ,®ú•¨ü ,±¥ªµ
.1987 ,©•®µ ¥• ,ù≤-´ù ≥£≤•ü• :∂ú≤ª†ù ,¥¢Æ¥™£°∂ª¥£ù¨

,©•®µ ¥• ,¥ú®†ú≤ª† ¥∂ß ,≥ª£† ∂≠•™¥° ∂§™®µ†† ,©ù•≤∂† :™Æù ©ü¥£ ,´®•ú ,¥£µ
.2000

•¥ù≥° ´£®∞ª ∂ü - ®ú¥µ• ±¥ú ∂Æü•®∂Æù∂ß :®ú•¥ú ,(¶¥°Æ) ¥®µ •®ú :¶ª∂ù ,©†¥ùú ,®ú§µ
.1996 ,©•®µ ¥• ,®ú•¥ú ©¥∞≠ ∂ú≤ª† ,®ú¥µ•-±¥úù ©•™®≠ª™©•µªü≥

.2002 ,©•®µ ¥• ,¥∂ß ∂ú≤ª†ù ,üª™®∂®¶•¥ü™´•üÆ±®¢¨••§µ

15 '™Æ ,1987 ,´û∂™¥ ,´®ú-¥ù ∂§•≠¥ù•¨ú :∂ú≤ª†ù ,©•¨ªß°©µ•ú ,¥¢Æ®ú ,¥§µ

.1992 ,†¨¨Æ¥ ,´ª£§•ù† ü¥µ™∂ú≤ª†ù ,≠ªü¥ª† ®µ ª∂ß®™©£¨™ ¥§µ

©•¥∂ú - ®ú¥µ• ±¥ú ∂Æü•®∂Æù∂ß : ®ú•¥ú ,(©ß¥°Æ) ¥®µ •®ú°¥û•ù ´ªÆüû :¶ª∂ù ,•®ú ,¥®µ
.1988 ,®ú•¥ú ©¥∞≠ ∂ú≤ª† ,®ú¥µ•-±¥úù ∂ª™≥™

.1975 ,ù•ùú ®ª ,ªù ©•¥ùü :¶ª∂ù ,∂•üª†•©™µ ∂ú¥•®µ ©•≠ª∞§ †µª®µ ,©µ¥û ,©ª®µ

®ßµ™:∂ú≤ª†ù ,†•∞ª∂ú ∂ªü†• ®µ •¨ªÆ¥†° •∂ß®† †™®Æ:†•∞ª∂ú®•¨•≠™ ,´ª¥µ ,©ª®µ
.2012 ,(©¥∞≠ ∂°Æü•)

.2015 ,´ª¥™µù ®ú•¥ú ∂§•≠¥ù•¨ú ∂ú≤ª† ,•∂ü •üª†•©¢•ß¥¨ú ,´°™ú ,ú¥•∞µ

±ªü•≥† ∂ú≤ª†ù ,≠¨••¥ ù≥Æ•≥£≤• ù¥† ®µ •¨£¥† °™®Æ®Æ:∂°¨ª≤° †ß®† ,∂ªü† ,Ø≠ª ,ú¥•∞µ
.2002 ,†¨¨Æ¥ ,ü£ªú™

:∂ú≤ª†ù ,∂•µú¥ù ¥∞≠ù ∂ªùú† ∂ªµ¥∞ù ©•¨ªÆ:∂ªùú† •≥¥∞ ,´°-´ù ®ú ª :¶ª∂ù ,®ù ª• ,ª®¥µ
.2003 ,∂°¨ªù∂

∂ªü¥∂† ,¶°•£† ü¥µ™∂ú≤ª†ù ,°¨¥ªüù •¨≠ ∂µ¥°™W °•™ù •ü¥£† ¶°•£† ,´•™ù ,•≥≠¨¥µ
.1999 ,©•®µ ¥• ,§¥ª∞≠†°

HELP US GET THE SECRET OUT!

If this book was a blessing to you in any way, please leave a positive rating and review at this page on Amazon (goodreads.com will also be great) *as the rabbis will try to flood the review section with negative comments to discourage people from reading it.*

It would also be a great blessing if you can SHARE the link to this book on your social media profile, to help get the truth out.

Thank you!
Eitan Bar and Golan Broshi

50198192R00063

Made in the USA
Columbia, SC
03 February 2019